BUILDING CUSTOM SOFTWARE TOOLS AND LIBRARIES

BUILDING CUSTOM SOFTWARE TOOLS AND LIBRARIES

Martin Stitt

John Wiley & Sons, Inc.
NEW YORK / CHICHESTER / BRISBANE / TORONTO / SINGAPORE

Library of Congress Cataloging-in-Publication Data

Stitt, Martin
    Building custom software tools and libraries / Martin Stitt.
      p. cm.
    Includes index.
    ISBN 0-471-57914-9 (alk. paper : disk). — ISBN 0-471-57915-7
(pbk.). — ISBN 0-471-57916-5 (disk)
    1. Computer software–Development. 2. Utilities (Computer programs). I. Title.
OA76.76.D47S47 1993
005.1—dc20   92-33072
                                         CIP

Printed in the United States of America
10 9 8 7 6 5 4 3 2 1

To my son, Jason, who loves life.

TRADEMARK ACKNOWLEDGMENTS

TASM, TLINK, and TLIB are registered trademarks of Borland International, Inc.

MASM, LINK, LIB, MS-DOS, and Windows are registered trademarks of Microsoft Corporation.

IBM, PC, XT, AT, and OS/2 are registered trademarks of International Business Machines Corporation.

BRIEF is a trademark of Solution Systems Company.

ABOUT THE AUTHOR

Martin Stitt began working as an electronics technician in 1972. His first brush with computers came when he designed and hand-built an 8080-based system. Martin progressed from there to work as a systems design engineer, developing microprocessor-based control systems for data communications, energy management, and data acquisition.

Martin now works as a contract software engineer and is involved in such projects as a multitasking/multiuser operating system, X.25, and NET-BIOS communications drivers, database applications, CASE systems, debugging tools, and, of course, library development.

His first book *Debugging: Creative Techniques and Tools for Software Repair,* was also published by John Wiley & Sons, Inc. He has written articles on software development published in *PC Tech Journal, Dr. Dobb's Journal, Computer Language, C User's Journal,* and *Tech Specialist.*

CONTENTS OVERVIEW

	Preface	xxi
1	Basic Tool Design	1
2	Basic Library Design	17
3	Language Issues	37
4	Building Tools	45
5	Building Libraries	81
6	Documentation Management	105
7	User Interfaces	115
8	File and Directory Processing	139
A	Pseudocode Conventions	167
B	C Source Code Listings	195
	On the Companion Diskette	265
	Index	267

CONTENTS

Preface   xxi

1 Basic Tool Design   1

Types of Tools   1
   The Standalone Utility   1
   The TSR   3
   The Device Driver   5
Modular Functions and Reusable Functions   6
   Designing for Modularity and Reusability   8
   Consequences   10
Filters and Pipes   11
Standalone Utilities versus Filters   14
   The Best of Both Worlds   15

2 Basic Library Design   17

Source/Include Libraries   17
   Resident Libraries   19
   Dynamic Link Libraries   22

Object Modules and Static-Link Libraries 22

Object Module Records 25

Linker Action for Object Modules and Libraries 27

Introduction to Link Order Control 31

3 Language Issues 37

Single-Language Programs 37

Mixing ASM Functions with an HLL Base 40

Mixing HLL Functions with an ASM Base 42

Summary of Language Models 43

4 Building Tools 45

The Template Files 45

GETSTOCK.BAT and Other Batch Files 46

Link Order Control for Tools 48

Resident/Nonresident Programming 51

Stack Issues 53

Stack Addressing with the BP Register 53

Stack Switching 56

A First-Cut Attempt 58

A Better Way 60

Accessing the Caller's Registers 66

Placing the Stack Switch Calls 68

The Stack Pocket Technique 70

TSR Specifics 70

Device Driver Specifics 72

The MODOBJ.EXE Utility 77

Using Other High-Level Languages 77

Stack Issues Revisited 77

5   Building Libraries   81

Identifying Library Candidates   81

An Example of Layering   82

Shell Processes   83

Designing Functions for Library Inclusion   83

Bottom-Up Design   84

Planning for Future Growth   84

Error Handling   86

Information Hiding, Encapsulation,
and Abstraction   87

Private and Public   88

Private Global Variables   88

Public Global Variables   90

Granularity   91

Private Helper Functions   91

Function Hooks   92

Video Driver Hooks   93

Getkeys Hooks   95

Function Hook Wrap-up   98

Testing Library Functions   98

Traditional Libraries and Link Order Control   99

Header Files   99

Generating a Library   100

Library Maintenance Tips   101

6   Documentation Management   105

EXTRACT.EXE—Basic Operation   106

Program Summary Comment Blocks   107

Library Function Comment Blocks   108

EXTRACT.EXE—Parameters 109

Running EXTRACT.EXE from a Library Makefile 112

7 User Interfaces 115

Command Line Parameter Parsing 115

Fixed-Position Parameters 115

Multiple File Specifications 116

Switch Parameters 117

Setting Up the Parsing Logic 119

Calling the Parsing Logic 124

Parsing Logic for Switches 125

Parsing Logic for Fixed Parameters 126

Parameter Defaults 127

Console Input Processing 128

The Polling Hook 131

The Filter Hook 131

Hook Function Interfacing 132

The Library Functions 132

Macro Peculiarities 133

Mouse Movement to Cursor Key Emulation 133

A Console Stack 135

Executing Multiple Threads 135

Coding for Reentrance 136

Interactions Between Hook Functions 136

8 File and Directory Processing 139

File Processing 140

Directory Processing 147

A Directory Search Library Module 148

The Need for List Building   151

Processing a Series of Source Files   153

Tree Processing   155

The Tree Structure   155

The `lc_build_tree()` Function   158

The `lc_trace_tree()` Function   158

The `lc_free_tree()` Function   161

Interconnections   161

Wildcard to Wildcard Transformations   162

Filter-Style File Processing   165

A   Pseudocode Conventions   167

Action Charts   167

Function Brackets   169

Logic Statement Constructs   170

Levels of Detail in Pseudocode   172

Simple Data Declarations   173

Structure Declarations   175

Arrays and Strings   176

Pointers and Hex Numbers   177

Function Declarations and Return Values   180

Operators and Readability   182

Controlling Execution Flow   186

Defined Constants and Reserved Variables   188

Comment Headers   188

Translation to Actual Code   190

B   C Source Listings   195

`lc_get_cmtail()`   195

`lc_get_ddtail()`   197 lc_rspfile()   198

lc_parse_sw()   200

lc_parse_fx()   206

lc_swp_assign()   210

lc_fxp_assign()   211

lc_isempty()   212

lc_trim_parm()   213

lc_inset()   214

lc_disp_char(), lc_disp_str(),
lc_disp_err_lead()   215

lc_setup_showsw(), lc_report_showsw()   217

lc_toupper()   219

lc_getchar()   220

lc_getfname()   222

lc_verify_hex_fx()   224

lc_verify_hex_sw()   225

lc_verify_hexstr()   227

lc_find_files()   229

lc_trace_dir()   232

free_lptr_list()   234

lc_trace_dirl()   235

lc_tracdir_prep()   239

lc_build_tree(), lc_trace_tree(),
lc_free_tree()   240

lc_eat_key()   248

lc_getkey_set()   249

lc_beep()   250

lc_set_phook(), lc_set_fhook(),
lc_set_ahook(), lc_getkey (),
lc_ifkey()   251

lc_process_src_parms()   255

lc_home_path()   258

lc_form_template(),
lc_translate_template()   259

lc_subst_meta()   262

On the Companion Diskette   265

Installing the Companion Toolset   265

Index   267

Chapter XIX

PREFACE

This is a book for those of you who need to write software utilities. You might be an engineer in need of a custom software tool to model the characteristics of a new design. You might be a scientist who requires a custom tool to interface a piece of prototype laboratory equipment. You might be a print-shop technician in need of a custom utility to translate foreign typesetting codes to your system. You may be a programmer in need of a custom tool to create data sets for an application you are testing. The possibilities are endless!

I wrote this book to show how custom software tooling can be created in an efficient manner.

This is not a book on "How to Program in Assembler" or "How to Program in C" (or in any other specific language, for that matter). Books of that sort are plentiful. Nor is it a book that presents a specific library of tool-building components, requiring you to wade through pages and pages of source code listings.

This book addresses the nuts-and-bolts issues involved in the design and implementation of custom tools, including the following:

- Different forms tools can take
- User interfaces
- System interfaces
- Tool-to-tool interfaces
- How compilation and linking work
- The design, construction, and maintenance of function libraries
- Documentation strategies for tools and library modules
- File processing

Library techniques are covered because they make reusable software possible. If you aren't familiar with the design and maintenance of a function library, then, as you build more and more tools, you either have to reinvent certain wheels or you end up using other, less efficient means to share code.

One of my goals in writing this book was to balance the presentation. When a book on software development is too general, readers must do additional research to attain knowledge that they can apply in their work. Conversely, a book with a narrow focus, such as just covering a certain language or specific brand of compiler, becomes dated quickly.

This book generalizes by presenting its program code in pseudocode form first. The action chart diagramming method is used to impart a graphic clarity to this pseudocode. This approach provides significant detail about the function of the software in an easy-to-read and language-independent manner. (See Appendix A for an explanation of this pseudocode method.)

Many of the pseudocode presentations are followed by an actual implementation in C or assembler. For your convenience, all code examined in this book is available in both source and binary form on the Companion Diskette.

A combination of C and assembler is used in the templates and library functions on the Companion Diskette. The C portions were developed in standard C using Borland C++ version 2.0; the assembler portions were developed using Microsoft's MASM 5.1 and are compatible with Borland's TASM.

The program templates are designed to produce drivers and utilities composed of various combinations of C and assembler code. Device drivers and TSRs can be written entirely in assembler or in a mixture of assembler and C. Stand-alone utility programs are supported as only assembler, only C, or a combination. The program library functions are available to all configurations.

Because of the generalized presentation of the code in the book, implementing this book's techniques in languages other than C should be an easy task. A working knowledge of the MS-DOS operating system and its system-level interface is presumed.

THE COMPANION LIBRARY

The Companion Library contains the following types of functions:

> Parsing Logic
>> Parse fixed and switch parameters
>> Support response files
> Console Input Processing
>> Get keys
>> Perform background processing while waiting for key input

Check key input for hot keys
Simulate key input
File Processing Logic
Read and process each line of a file
Find first and find next file in a directory
Traverse directory tree on a disk
Stack-Switching Logic
Switch to local stack
Switch back to caller's stack
Pass call on to previous vector holder
String/Memory Logic
Copy blocks of memory
Fill memory
Copy/fill strings
Measure the length of strings
Check for character inclusion in a string
Display Logic
Display characters and strings
I/O Logic
Input a byte from a port
Output a byte to a port
Conversion Logic
Convert binary to decimal ASCII
Convert binary to hexadecimal ASCII
Convert text ASCII to hexadecimal
Convert character to upper case
Miscellaneous Logic
Derive a program's home path
Enable and disable interrupts

BUILDING CUSTOM SOFTWARE TOOLS AND LIBRARIES

CHAPTER 1
Basic Tool Design

In this chapter we'll take a look at some of the basic aspects of tool design. Because building tools and libraries are often interdependent practices, you'll find that this chapter on tool design also discusses libraries and the chapters on library design cover the construction and design of tools as well.

This may seem like a lot of bouncing back and forth. At times, it may even seem like we're building a house both from the ground up and from the top down. In fact, that is precisely what is being done, such is the nature of interdependence.

TYPES OF TOOLS

The Standalone Utility

The standalone utility is the most familiar and common form of program. Most likely, you have used this type of program many times. Its code and data are contained within a file of the .COM or .EXE type. If you've assembled or compiled the obligatory "Hello world" sample program in your favorite language, then you've already made a standalone utility.

Standalone programs can be invoked manually from the command line or from within a batch file, or they can be executed as a child process of another utility program, such as a command shell, that allows you to start programs by pointing to their name in a list or by clicking on an icon. This type of tool can be as simple as the TREE utility included with MS-DOS, or it can be a more interactive tool—one that presents menus and prompts such as a spreadsheet or a CAD package. This book focuses on the development of smaller tools, but the techniques presented will also be valuable in larger-scale projects.

Some examples of smaller scale standalone utilities include the following:

- A print-formatting program
- A sort utility
- A text file filter
- A text file translation utility
- A data file generator
- A data file conversion tool
- A data file dumper/browser
- A testbed environment for flexing a function
- A disk maintenance tool that displays a directory tree; deletes, un-deletes, moves, or copies files; and so on.

When this type of utility is to be executed, the MS-DOS EXEC logic loads the program's initial code and data into memory from the .COM or .EXE file. Once this loading is complete, the EXEC logic "jumps into" the newly loaded program, transferring all execution control to it. The MS-DOS operating system code and data remain in memory (providing the utility doesn't errantly overwrite it) and are thus available to fulfill requests from the utility for file and console I/O services.

In an MS-DOS type environment, where the operating system kernel is actually more of an I/O service provider than an operating system, the utility, while it is running, has near total control of the machine. It can program hardware directly and access all available memory. Of course, the utility must not overwrite the actual code and data of MS-DOS, or a crash will occur.

The standalone type of program is also called a transient program. The memory area where such programs are loaded is called the transient program area (TPA). Once a transient program's operations are complete, it returns control of the system to the MS-DOS command processor and gives up any claims it had on the system's memory.

This type of program can be produced from one or more source code modules written in assembler, in a high-level language, or in a mixture of both. For pure assembler programs, programmers either write each and every line or they use some of their own code plus some ready-made library code developed by a third party.

When a program is written in a high-level language, the resulting binary module is made up of code translated not only from the programmer's statements but also from additional support code that is part of the high-level language package. The first piece of this support code is the initialization logic that checks for sufficient memory and performs other tasks to set the stage for the user-written code. Other parts of this supporting substratum deal with error handling, exception processing, overlay management, and program termination.

For programs developed in a high-level language, it is also very common for functions to be bound into the binary module from a library. These functions may be included in the language's standard library, or they may be from third-party library packages, or both. It is even possible for programs written in a high-level language to be linked with modules written in another language, such as assembler.

The TSR

The terminate and stay resident (TSR) type of utility is like the relative who comes for a visit and never leaves. This type of tool loads into the TPA just like a transient program, but when it terminates back to MS-DOS, it specifies that a portion of the TPA it occupies be retained for later use.

Here are some examples of TSR utilities:

- The pop-up notepad, phone dialer, calculator
- A keyboard macro utility
- A background printing utility
- A print-screen replacement that captures screen data in a file
- An interface driver for a CD-ROM drive or other special type of storage unit
- A binary tree file service module
- A background communications tool
- An interface driver for a mouse
- An interface to a LAN

When loaded, TSR utilities typically establish some means for communication, usually through an interrupt intercept. Many TSRs intercept the INT09 and INT16 keyboard interrupts. The timer interrupts INT08 and INT1C are also common choices. Other interrupts could be intercepted depending on the TSR's function. For example, a background printing utility would likely establish an intercept of the INT17 BIOS printing services interrupt.

A properly structured TSR contains two distinct sections of code: a resident section and a nonresident section (see Figure 1.1). When a TSR is loaded into memory, it is the nonresident section that receives control first. Some of the functions typically undertaken by the nonresident section are as follows:

- Check for sufficient memory
- Check the MS-DOS version number

```
            ┌──────────────────────────┐
            │       TSR Utility        │
      ┌─────┴──────────────────────────┴─────┐
      │  Nonresident section:                 │
      │    code and data that                 │
      │    verifies parameters,               │
      │    initializes the                    │
      │    resident logic, and                │
      │    invokes the resident               │
      │    type of termination.               │
      │                                       │
      ├───────────────────────────────────────┤
      │                                       │
      │  Resident section:                    │
      │    code and data that                 │
      │    remain resident in                 │
      │    memory.                            │
      │                                       │
      └───────────────────────────────────────┘
```

FIGURE 1.1   Resident/nonresident layout for a TSR.

- Process any command line parameters
- Initialize data within the resident section
- Load any required data files into memory
- Display signon messages
- Determine the resident section's size
- Terminate, specifying the amount of memory to be retained

Once the nonresident section has set the stage for the resident part, the memory initially occupied by the nonresident section can be reused by other utilities and application programs that are loaded into the TPA.

To return to the visiting-relative analogy, once these uninvited kin have unpacked, they send their empty luggage back home. Count your blessings, though; it's better than having them send for their furniture!

Note that although it is possible to develop TSR tools in a high-level language, special considerations are required. First, the standard startup and termination code that compilers bond into the programs they produce are designed for transient type programs. This startup and termination logic must either be modified or totally replaced to accommodate the TSR type of termination method.

Second, many restrictions exist regarding the type of operating system calls the resident section can make. In many cases it is not wise to use any of the standard library functions that are normally part of a high-level language.

Third, high-level languages typically do not allow you to isolate the code and data that should make up the nonresident section in one area at the end of the module. This restriction is especially troublesome when library functions are linked into the program that will be used by the resident portion. Library modules are typically added on to the end of the initial code module.

Most books and journal articles that describe the construction of TSRs in a high-level language present a crude "ballpark" approach to memory allocation. No attempt is made to isolate resident code and data from nonresident, and the derivation of how much memory will be required for the final resident load is based on a trial-and-error approach.

This book does not cover the many issues involved in TSR construction, such as operating system reentrance, compatibility problems with other TSRs, and how to remove a TSR from memory. What it will cover is how to develop TSRs in assembler, in a high-level language, or in a mixture of the two, and how to retain full control over the placement of the resident and nonresident code and data. Finally, this book will cover the design of a library system that ensures that library functions used by the resident section are linked into the resident section and that functions used by the nonresident section are linked into that section.

The Device Driver

A device driver is a code module that is installed as part of the MS-DOS operating system when a computer boots up. Its primary purpose is to isolate the kernel from the specific hardware in a given computer system. This module must conform to a specific interface standard to provide responses to requests made of it by the MS-DOS kernel.

Some examples of hardware devices that often require a device driver are as follows:

- A tape backup unit
- Nonstandard types of disk drives such as CD-ROM and WORM drives
- A mouse, digitizer tablet, or bar-code scanner
- A nonstandard type of printer
- A network interface adapter

Device drivers can also provide services without interfacing directly with an external hardware peripheral. RAM disk drivers (e.g., RAMDRIVE.SYS) and disk-caching drivers (e.g., SMARTDRV.SYS) provide disk emulation and disk enhancement services without interfacing directly to any specific hardware. Another type is the memory management driver (e.g., HIMEM.SYS).

Just as with the TSR, a properly configured device driver is made up of a resident section and a nonresident section. (See Figure 1.2.) The nonresident

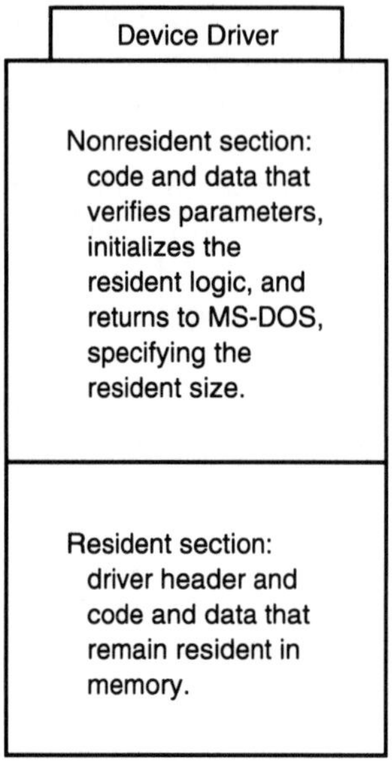

```
┌─────────────────────────────┐
│      Device Driver          │
├─────────────────────────────┤
│                             │
│   Nonresident section:      │
│     code and data that      │
│     verifies parameters,    │
│     initializes the         │
│     resident logic, and     │
│     returns to MS-DOS,      │
│     specifying the          │
│     resident size.          │
│                             │
├─────────────────────────────┤
│                             │
│   Resident section:         │
│     driver header and       │
│     code and data that      │
│     remain resident in      │
│     memory.                 │
│                             │
│                             │
└─────────────────────────────┘
```

FIGURE 1.2   Resident/nonresident layout for a device driver.

section receives control first and is charged with tasks such as

- Parsing any 'device=' line parameters
- Testing and initializing the hardware device being interfaced
- Initializing data within the resident section
- Displaying signon messages
- Determining the resident section's size
- Returning to MS-DOS, specifying the amount of memory to be retained

It is also possible to write device drivers in a high-level language such as C. Although this is not a book on how to write device drivers, it will cover the pertinent issues of resident and nonresident section isolation, proper memory allocation control, and how to design a library system that cooperates with this sectioning scheme.

MODULAR FUNCTIONS AND REUSABLE FUNCTIONS

This book uses the term *module* when referring to a file containing a program's source code or executable binary code. We will now begin to use the term *modular* as an attribute of the individual functions within a program.

In both cases, the idea is the same—to suggest that the code's purpose, implementation, and interface be clearly defined. (Note that the terms *function, subprocedure, subroutine,* and *procedure* are considered equivalent for the purposes of this discussion.)

Rigorous application of modular principles produces the greatest benefit at the level of the individual function. So what precisely is a modular function? In short, a modular function is a self-contained unit of code and data that performs a distinct function, has a well-defined interface and can be understood easily by itself.

What is meant by the term *reusable*? Often, functions are called from more than one point within a program. In a sense, all such functions could then be considered reusable within the realm of their mother program. Benefits really accrue, though, when a function's design and implementation allow it to be used in more than one program. Therefore, our definition of a reusable function is one that can be used in more than one program.

Although it is certainly advantageous for a function to be reusable as well as modular, modularity alone does not guarantee reusability. A reusable function should certainly be modular, but these two attributes do not always have a reciprocal relationship. Many of the functions within a program will be so application specific that reusability is simply not a practical consideration.

The basic message of this book is to strive for modularity in all functions and reusability in as many as possible. Further, whenever reusability is possible, the function should be implanted in a library as soon as possible. Consequently, the terms *reusable function* and *library function* will be considered synonymous from here on.

"Why do this?" you ask. "What exactly are these benefits?"

Benefits of Modular Functions

1. When each function is clearly defined and documented, the program is easier to understand as a whole. To make use of an IF/ELSE statement within a high-level language rarely requires that you study the assembler code that the compiler will generate. Likewise, with a properly designed and documented modular function, you can understand how it is used and how it can be used without having to analyze its code line by line.

2. A modular function can be rewritten to use a better algorithm or to execute the current algorithm faster (e.g., by rewriting it in assembler or by taking advantage of a coprocessor). If a function's implementation is changed but its interface is not, there should be no need for any adjustments in any other part of the program.

3. Modular functions can be tested and debugged more easily within a testbed environment. Therefore, programs built from modular functions will have fewer bugs themselves.

4. Porting a program made up of modular functions is easier. The parts that are specific to a certain machine, operating system, or compiler can be isolated to a small group of well-defined functions.
5. In a large project with a team of programmers, the workload can be split up more easily since the details of different functions are hidden from other parts of the program. Also, more capable team members can be assigned the more complex functions.

Benefits of Reusable Functions

1. All reusable functions are to be modular first, and thus all the advantages listed for modular functions apply here.
2. You get more mileage out of your development effort.
3. Using precompiled library modules speeds the compilation of the programs you build using such libraries.
4. When you want to build a testbed for future parts of a project, having many of the building block functions already in a library greatly simplifies the setup of the testbed.
5. A library of reusable functions can be made into a salable product.

Designing for Modularity and Reusability

During the design and coding of a utility program or a full-scale applications package, many opportunities will arise for the creation of reusable functions. By learning how to design functions to be reusable and by learning how to construct, use, and maintain libraries of these functions, the benefits listed earlier can be yours.

Although a detailed treatment of this topic must wait until Chapter 5, we need to take an introductory look at it here because the topics of tool design and library design are interrelated; to discuss one often requires that the other be discussed as well.

Does placing a section of code within a function automatically make it a modular function? Absolutely not! Is it possible to make all functions modular? That's debatable.

A group of statements is often turned into a function because that group is used at more than one location within a program. Although eliminating redundant coding is beneficial, it doesn't guarantee modularity. These common statements may make significant use of global variables, or they may be very poorly structured, branching into other units of code or being branched into by other parts of a program.

The key factors are as follows:

• Comprehensive documentation
• Distinct purpose and behavior (cohesion)

- Interdependence and isolation (coupling)
- Clearly defined entry and exit data

For modularity to succeed, clear documentation is a must. You can begin by writing a description of each function's operation and interface (entry and exit parameters, use of global variables). Then step back and pretend you don't know anything about each function's implementation. Is what you've written clear enough to allow you to make use of the function? Once you've refined this description to pass your own scrutiny, seek a peer's review. (Chapter 6 presents more information on documentation management.)

Cohesion is a measure of how related the operations within a function or module are. As long as the overall purpose and behavior of a function remains distinct and the interface remains clearly defined, it is acceptable to handle a group of related operations within the same function. When a function's operations are not closely related, it is said to have a low degree of cohesion—an undesirable attribute for a modular design.

Coupling is a measure of the interdependence between a specific function and other functions or between that specific function and other parts of the program in which it is being used. A high degree of operational isolation between a function and the other parts of a program is always desirable. This would be called a low degree of coupling.

Isolation between different aspects of a program can be applied at more than one level. It can be applied at a higher, more abstract level by requiring that the functions constituting the data-processing "guts" of a program be totally oblivious to those that support the user interface. The benefits of this approach to porting between different operating platforms should be obvious. At a lower level, requiring that the user interface input logic be highly isolated from the user interface output logic can be helpful. This isolation can simplify the adaptation of a keyboard-based program to alternate input devices such as a mouse or pen device.

At an even more detailed level, it is important to design each function within a group to have a high degree of isolation (a low degree of coupling). When one function passes only data to another function, that second function is able to interpret the data by any means available based on the function's design. But when one function passes a control flag to another, the actions carried out by that second function are being controlled in a very direct manner by its caller. This lack of isolation can make a program more difficult to maintain, because changes in one function can affect the operation of another.

Another area where the idea of isolation should be considered is in the use of global data. There are certain situations where the use of global variables does make good sense, but unless they are approached with great care, their use is an invitation for maintenance problems.

When global data is used throughout a program without clear control you cannot completely understand the behavior of one function without researching the other uses of the global data it depends on. This often means that you must understand the behavior of other functions first—and when they also use global data . . . madness.

In what kinds of situations are global references acceptable? A prime example would be for the type of data derived once during a program's startup phase and then used only for reference from then on. For instance, when a program is first loaded, it reads the contents of a configuration file into a set of global variables. These variables dictate feature choices such as the address of the display driver to use, the color attributes to use for different types of messages, the type of peripherals connected (e.g., printer, mouse, modem), and so on. Again, Chapter 5 will take a closer look at these ideas as well as calling hierarchy (layering and inheritance), use of parameters and local and global variables (data abstraction and information hiding), function granularity, and error handling. The primary focus of Chapter 5 is on developing functions for inclusion into a library, which means functions that are both modular and reusable. This material can also be useful when designing modular functions that are application specific if you remain aware of the distinction.

Consequences

When you create functions that are close to being reusable and then go on to use these functions in your program in their current state, you are building a significant obstacle to their ultimate placement within a library. The "I'll go back later and make these into library modules" approach is rarely practical. The time pressures of project completion don't allow for this.

In order for the "go back and do it later" approach to work, you would have to do the following:

1. Modify the functions to be fully reusable
2. Move them into a library
3. Test the functions in their library form
4. Modify all parts of each program affected by this rewriting and relocation
5. Retest each affected program

By developing candidate functions as library modules in the first place, you'll save yourself a lot of time in the long run. True, you'll still have to go through the first three steps listed above, but the time saved when steps 4 and 5 are bypassed can be significant. In addition, you will begin to reap the benefits of having these functions in a library all that much sooner.

The best way to implement this approach is to be prepared to build libraries from the start of your next project—which is what this book is all about.

FILTERS AND PIPES

A filter is a program that accepts a stream of input data and emits a corresponding stream of output data after having performed some type of processing on that stream. This is much like the air filter in a car's engine, except that the definition of "clean air" is programmable. The FIND utility, provided with MS-DOS, is a prime example.

In addition to filtering a data stream, where the output is a select subset of the input, a filter utility can also manipulate the data stream in other ways. For example, rather than reducing the amount of data, the MS-DOS SORT utility reorders it. Filters can also be made that will transform the data stream in other ways, such as converting tabs to spaces and uppercase text to lowercase. Encryption and decryption of a data stream can also be done.

If a program uses either standard input (stdin) or standard output (stdout), redirection may be used. How do you know when a program uses these input and output channels? In most cases, a program that doesn't produce its display using full screen addressing does use stdout. To make sure, you can try an experiment such as the following:

```
utilprog > output.txt
```

If you end up with an empty file and see the normal output on the display, then this program is using some other means to produce its display (e.g., writing to stderr, calling the BIOS, or writing directly to the display adapter's memory).

You can also try this type of experiment on the input side by creating a file that contains an input script suitable to the program being tested. Just be sure to include the commands necessary to terminate the program, or your system will be hung up.

```
utilprog < input.txt
```

The stdin and stdout channels can be thought of as channels through which a utility receives its input and through which its output is funneled. (See Figure 1.3.) The default source for the stdin channel is the keyboard and the default destination for the stdout channel is the main video display.

Figure 1.4 shows the type of redirection that would be in effect when the DIR command is used with output redirection. Note that as soon as the DIR command completes, the output file is closed and the stdout channel is restored to its default state, in which the video display is used as the destination.

In Figure 1.5 the DIR command is being used in a pipeline arrangement with the standalone utility FIND.COM. The MS-DOS command processor orchestrates pipelining by executing the internal command or utilities one at a

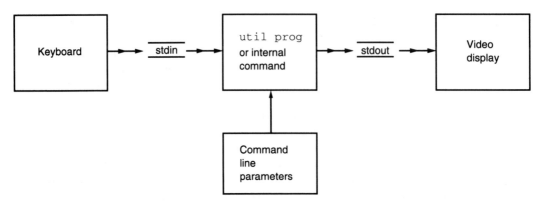

FIGURE 1.3 Basic process model for stdin and stdout channels.

time, in serial order, using temporary files. The temporary file that captures the stdout data from one process is used as the stdin source for the next process in the chain.

The use of input redirection is illustrated in Figure 1.6. The contents of the file PAT01 are fed to the DEBUG utility program in place of normal keyboard input. Through a command-line parameter, DEBUG is made to load the file XYZ.COM. It is on this file that the operations within the patch script, PAT01, will operate.

A script file of this type would typically contain instructions to invoke DEBUG's immediate assembler or to use its e command (enter) to poke new data into the memory image of the file being patched. The script would conclude with a w command (write) to update this modified memory image to the disk file and then a q command to cause DEBUG.COM to terminate.

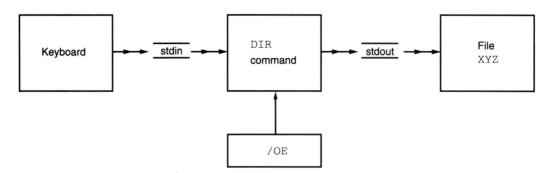

FIGURE 1.4 Result of DIR /OE > XYZ.

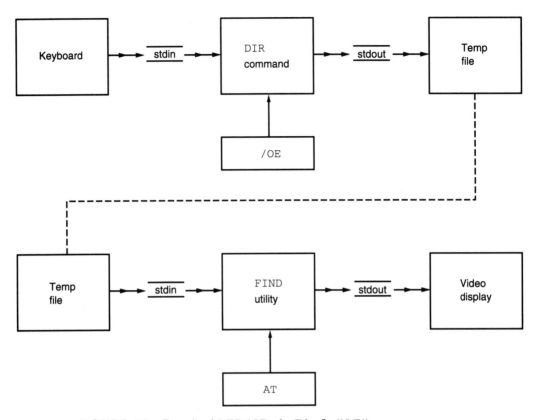

FIGURE 1.5 Result of `DIR/OE ¦ Find "AT"`.

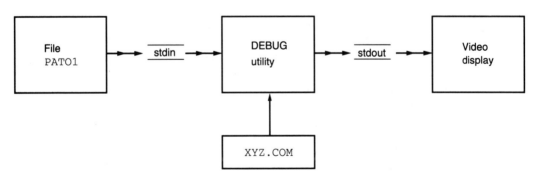

FIGURE 1.6 Result of `DEBUG XYZ.COM < PAT01`.

STANDALONE UTILITIES VERSUS FILTERS

Using filter type utilities in a pipeline arrangement applies modularity and reusability at the program level. Having a library of modular and reusable functions gives you the same opportunities at the program level. Instead of designing a command line, often enclosed within a batch file, you write a program.

Both methods have their advantages and disadvantages, so it's good to be familiar with each in order to choose the best approach for each situation.

Advantages of Pipelining

- You end up with a collection of well-defined utilities—programs that are modular and reusable.
- Each utility can be tested as a whole unit. Once it passes this testing, the chance of bugs arising from different usage combinations is small.
- Pipelining can be used in conjunction with existing utilities and internal commands. You can modify and enhance the actions of internal commands such as DIR.
- If sufficient pipeline-oriented utilities are available, and you are familiar with their use, you can develop processes spontaneously at the command line.
- These smaller and simpler utility programs are typically easier to build and debug.

Disadvantages of Pipelining

- Processing options are limited. The stdin and stdout channels are designed only for text-based data. Processing a binary stream is not practical. Further, the order of processing is a serial, first-to-last type of sequence. Iteration is only possible through batch file contrivances—which are limited and slow.
- Extra processing time is required for each utility to be loaded into memory for execution and for intermediate data to be written to and read from temporary files.
- Pipelining will only work with utilities designed to read from stdin and write to stdout.
- The number of input sources is limited to the number supported by the first utility in the chain, and the number of final output destinations is limited to the number supported by the last utility used in the chain.

Advantages of Writing a New Program for Each Case

- It is possible to highly customize the program code to the process.
- Much more processing can be done in a given amount of time.
- Much more complex types of data manipulation can be performed.
- Manipulations can be done on binary data, and operations can be iterative and recursive.
- User interface options are wide open. Utilities can be interactive.
- Multiple input sources and output destinations can be used.
- The design and construction of custom utilities provides many opportunities to add reusable functions to your libraries.
- You gain more programming experience from working with larger, more complex utilities.

Disadvantages of Writing a New Program for Each Case

- Time is required to design, code, test and debug, each new program.

The Best of Both Worlds

In certain cases, it is possible to design a utility to have a split personality, where it can be used either as a filter or as a standalone program. The MS-DOS FIND utility has been designed this way. If a filename parameter is included on the command line, then the input data stream is taken from the named file rather than the stdin stream. When no filename parameter is specified, the input data stream is expected to come from the stdin channel.

CHAPTER 2
Basic Library Design

This chapter will examine different approaches to library construction. Although knowledge of object module internals is not required to build your own libraries, a familiarity with this topic can be helpful when it comes to optimization and the diagnosis of linker errors.

SOURCE/INCLUDE LIBRARIES

Although include files are frequently used in software development, they are ill suited for forming software function libraries. Include files are good for header data: function prototypes, macros, definition of common constants, and similar overhead constructs. This section will expose the weaknesses of the include file library method to help you appreciate the benefits of the more capable methods.

Figure 2.1 illustrates the processing of an include file during a compilation. The preprocessor section of the compiler package reads each line of your source file, watching for statements containing the include keyword (assembler uses include, C uses #include). When this keyword is encountered, the preprocessor locates and opens the named include file and produces a temporary file containing the sum total of the source file and the include file.

This process could also be extended to accommodate multiple include statements within the source file or nested include statements within an include file. Note also that this is a general model—whenever possible, the compiler may simply merge all files directly within RAM rather than create a temporary file.

If you have functions in transition, using include files as a library vehicle can be beneficial. When you are first developing a set of functions that will eventually be moved into a more permanent type of library, it can be helpful to begin with the include file method as it is very simple to set up.

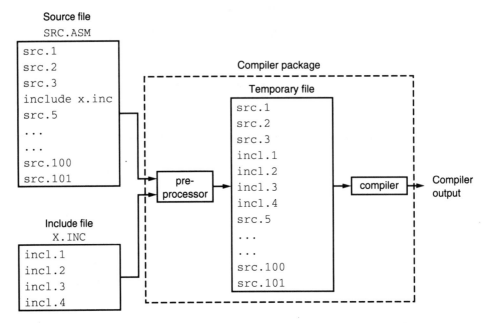

FIGURE 2.1 How the preprocessor merges source and include files.

During a program's alpha-testing phase, when debugging is a prevalent activity, having the source code for these transitional functions compiled directly with the main source code makes it easier to produce debugging information in a .MAP file or in the final .EXE file. This information tells a debugger which line in the source file corresponds to which address within the executable binary module. Source-level debugging requires this type of correspondence data.

The drawbacks to this method are plentiful:

- Extra compile time is required for each build of a program.
- You must specify the location of the include files to the compiler. This creates a maintenance hassle when development is done on different machines with different directory structures.
- Granularity problems can easily occur. If you build one large include file, then a program that only uses a few functions is bloated by all the functions it does not need. If you produce a number of smaller include files, you must keep track of the function-calling hierarchy— which include file functions require the inclusion of other include files.
- An include file library system won't support modules produced from different languages as other library methods will.
- When include files must declare global variables, the placement of the include statement within the main source file may be critical. Some

compilers must find all global variable declarations before any functions, which means placing the include statement just after all global declarations in the main source module and before any functions are defined. When more than one include file requires this type of placement, you must then split the include files.

- Private global variables are not possible. Any global variables within an include file become part of the main program, which may cause name conflicts. With other library forms, variables can be declared that are global to the family of functions within a library module but are not visible outside that module.

Resident Libraries

A resident library is typically packaged as a TSR type of program. External access to the set of library functions is usually achieved through the use of an interrupt vector. Figure 2.2 shows one way a resident library might be used.

In this scenario, a batch file such as the one following is used to activate the application. This batch file first loads the TSR library module into memory (named RTLIB.EXE in this example) and then invokes the application (named APP.EXE). When the application terminates, the last line of this batch file invokes the RTLIB.EXE TSR program with a /U switch parameter, causing the TSR to unload itself.

The batch file RUN_APP.BAT:

```
rtlib
app
rtlib /u
```

In Figure 2.2, the term TPA refers to the transient program area, the region of memory where MS-DOS loads TSRs and application programs. In step *a,* the batch is loading the resident library, RTLIB.EXE, into the TPA. In step *b* the batch file is loading the application, APP.EXE, into the TPA.

Step *c* shows the APP.EXE program loaded in memory and making use of the resident library functions. Additional free memory within the TPA is used for data and stack. In *d* the APP.EXE program has just terminated, leaving only the resident library in memory. Finally, in *e* the last line of the batch file executes, causing the RTLIB.EXE TSR to unload itself from memory.

In the real world, refinements would be called for. The TSR should check for a prior load of itself, and the batch file should check for an ERRORLEVEL after loading the TSR (to manage errors such as insufficient memory, prior

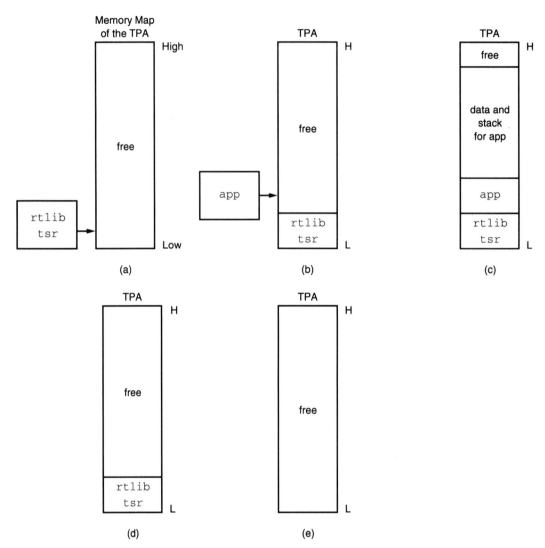

FIGURE 2.2 Loading/unloading steps for a TSR-style resident library.

load, and so on). A signature at a defined offset from the interrupt handler's entry point is often used as a means for a TSR to verify prior loading.

Figure 2.3 shows a variation on the resident library scheme. Instead of being packaged as an independent TSR type program, the library module is configured as an overlay module. This overlay is loaded into memory through the execution of code within each application that uses the library. For resident libraries provided with a compiler, the compiler will automatically add startup code to the application to perform this loading.

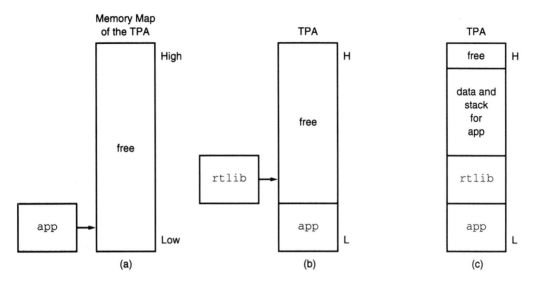

FIGURE 2.3 Loading/unloading steps for an overlay-style resident library.

This method can also be used to load in your own library overlay—where you would add specific code to your application to perform the overlay loading process. The application can make calls to this overlay module by using a predefined offset within the module as an entry point. Because the application loaded the overlay into memory, the overlay's location in memory is known to it. An interrupt vector could also be used.

Because the portion of the TPA memory used by the library module was allocated by the application, the module's memory will automatically be freed when the application terminates.

The advantages of the resident library approach are as follows:

- If you change a function, all programs that use the library are instantly affected.
- The binary file for each program that uses this type of library can be smaller. When the library is retained in memory, each program will load and begin execution in less time.
- You can build one of these libraries in stages. You can put together the functions in quick and simple style at first so you can get on with building the programs that use the library. You can then rewrite the library code later to be more efficient. When using this technique, carefully consider the calling interface of each library function, padding entry and exit structure parameters with reserved fields or defining certain CPU registers as reserved (for the ASM case).

The disadvantages are as follows:

- Memory must be allocated for the entire library even when a program will only use a few of its functions.
- The resident library is one more file that must be distributed and installed.
- More operational steps are required to load the library module. Issues such as insufficient memory and file not found errors must be dealt with at one more point.

Dynamic Link Libraries

Dynamic link libraries (DLLs) are used by the Microsoft Windows operating environment and IBM's OS/2 operating system. This form of library is very similar to the resident library described above in that the code and data for each library is contained within a separate binary module. The main difference is that the operating environment automatically manages the loading and unloading of library modules.

A model of this process is shown in Figure 2.4. Windows maintains a memory pool for applications and another for DLLs. When a windows application is loaded, it specifies the DLL modules it requires (Figure 2.4a). Windows then locates and loads each library module into memory (Figure 2.4b).

One interesting feature of the DLL approach is that multiple applications can be loaded in a multitasking configuration where each shares one copy of the DLL program code. In that situation, the operating system automatically allocates and manages instance-specific data areas.

When an application terminates, any DLLs that were loaded for it will automatically be unloaded from memory. In the case where multiple applications are sharing a DLL, this unloading will not occur until the last application terminates.

OBJECT MODULES AND STATIC-LINK LIBRARIES

As shown in Figure 2.5, when a source code file is processed by a compiler, a file of the .OBJ type results. Rather than producing pure machine code directly, a compiler generates a file, known as an *object module,* that contains the code and data in an intermediate form. The object module file generated from a given source-code module typically has the same filename as that source module but uses the .OBJ extension (e.g., assembling XYZ.ASM produces XYZ.OBJ; compiling ABC.C produces ABC.OBJ). This same intermediate form of output is also generated by an assembler.

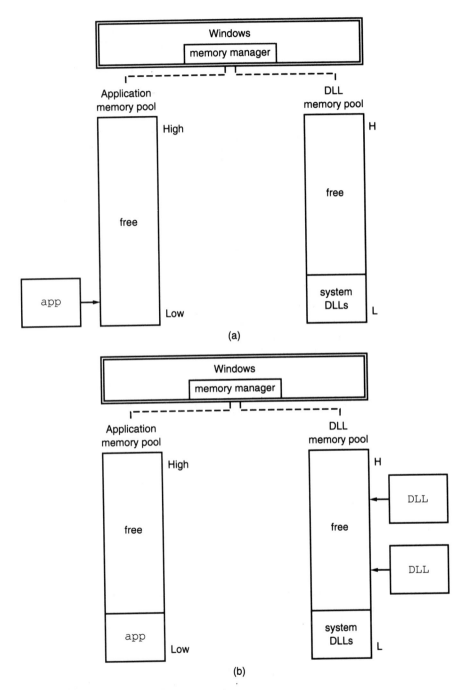

FIGURE 2.4   DLL operations in Windows.

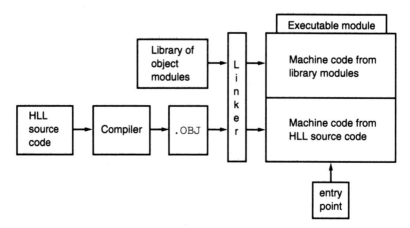

FIGURE 2.5   The compile and link process.

An .OBJ file contains one object module; thus, for all practical purposes, these two terms are synonymous and will be used interchangeably throughout this book. Although some operating environments may support multiple object modules per .OBJ file, the rule in MS-DOS is 1:1.

The main reason compilers and assemblers produce code and data in this intermediate form is to make it possible to build a program from multiple-source code modules. Were a compiler or assembler to produce its output in the form of pure machine code, there would be no practical way to link together separate files of this pure code to form one larger program. Each source code file would have to contain the instructions for each and every function that was required.

While object modules do contain machine code and binary program data, they also contain instructions that enable the linker to build a larger executable program module from one or more pieces. Each of these pieces would be an object module that was generated from a separate source file. The next section will look at the composition of object modules in detail.

A static-link library is basically a collection of object modules contained within a file of the type .LIB. Figure 2.5 shows a basic model of the compilation process involving the linking of an .OBJ file and object modules from a library. The final result is a standalone program of the .EXE type.

The linker is the chief player in the processing of both individual .OBJ files and static-link libraries. The linker examines the object module produced by the compiler and determines which library functions are referenced. The linker then locates each of these functions within the library and binds them into the final .EXE file, along with the main program code and data from the standalone .OBJ file.

The linking process is the same when an assembler is used instead of a compiler. For sake of simplicity, this basic model ignores the issues of startup code, multiple object modules, and multiple libraries. (These issues will be discussed later.)

When static-link libraries are used, even though the library specified to the linker may contain hundreds of individual object modules, the resulting .EXE file contains only the library functions that are actually needed by the program. This method of library development will be studied in great detail elsewhere in this book.

OBJECT MODULE RECORDS

This section will take a brief look at the internal makeup of an object module. Although it is not necessary to fully understand machine code generation in order to develop and use libraries, a basic understanding of object module processing is good to have. It will not only enhance your ability to create useful libraries, but when you're undertaking a large, multi-module project and your linker reports errors such as "unresolved external" and "fixup overflow," you will be able to find a solution much more easily.

An object module is a file that contains a combination of two types of information:

1. Partially processed binary data and machine code instructions
2. Information that tells the linker how to complete the processing of that binary code and data in order to produce an executable module

In order for a program's binary code and data to be fully ready for execution, all jumps, calls, and data references between the different parts of the program must be fully resolved based on the final position of each function and each block of data within the executable module. The linker is the program development tool charged with this resolution. For the linker to do its job, it must be told the location of each point within each object module that needs further processing and exactly what type of processing must be done.

Table 2.1 lists the name of each type of record along with a description of its use. If you own a Borland language product, you can use their TDUMP.EXE utility to examine the record structure of an object module. You should also find object module dumping utilities on bulletin boards and from programmer's shareware services.

Figure 2.6 shows the record structure of a typical object module. Be aware that most of these records are of variable length. For example, the size

Table 2.1   Object module records

Place-marker Records	
THEADR	*Translator HEADer Record:* always the first record in an object module; contains the name of the source file from which the object module was produced
MODEND	*MODule END record:* always the last record in an object module
Inter-module Linkage Records	
EXTDEF	*EXTernal DEFinition record:* identifies symbols (names of variables, functions, or branch entry points) that are referenced within the object module but do not exist within the module
PUBDEF	*PUBlic DEFinition record:* identifies symbols (names of variables, functions, or branch entry points) within the object module that are to be made available to other object modules
TYPDEF	*TYPe DEFinition record:* qualifies an EXTDEF or PUBDEF record by describing the symbol's data type
Name and Segment Definition Records	
LNAMES	*List of NAMES record.* contains a list of text strings that are referenced by SEGDEF and GRPDEF records
SEGDEF	*SEGment DEFinition record:* contains information about a program segment
GRPDEF	*GRouP DEFinition record:* contains information about a grouping relationship for program segments
Code and Data Records	
LEDATA	*Logical Enumerated DATA record:* contains executable binary program code and binary program data
LIDATA	*Logical Iterated DATA record:* contains executable binary program code and binary program data of a repeating nature
Miscellaneous Records	
FIXUPP	*FIXUP record:* contains information required to adjust address values within the object module's binary code and data
COMMENT	*COMMENT record:* contains information that may be used by the linker, the library utility or a debugger
COMDEF	*COMmunal names DEFinition record:* declares communal variables – variables that are shared by multiple modules in a common data area
LINNUM	*LINe NUMber record:* associates code offsets with source-file line numbers; used to effect source-level debugging

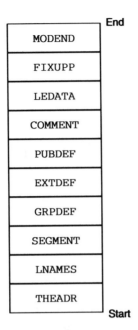

FIGURE 2.6 Structure of a typical object module.

of an LNAMES record depends on the number and length of the strings used to name a program's segments, groups, and segment classes. Similarly, the size of an LEDATA record depends on the amount of binary code and data it represents. This could be only a few bytes for a small module to thousands of bytes for a larger one.

Note also that you won't find each type of record in each object module. Whereas the THEADR and MODEND records are essential, others such as LIDATA and COMDEF will only appear in certain modules. It all depends on the language statements from which the object module is generated and the design of the compiler or assembler being used.

LINKER ACTION FOR OBJECT MODULES AND LIBRARIES

When a linker processes one or more object modules, it melds together the code and data based on the segment structure defined by the SEGDEF and GRPDEF records. The linker builds internal tables to track address reference points in the code and then seeks to resolve each one. An error message is generated for each point that cannot be resolved.

At minimum, you must specify one object module to the linker. It is also possible to link multiple explicit object modules and to specify one or more libraries full of object modules. The name of the .EXE file that the linker will produce defaults to the name of the first .OBJ file if no other specification is made.

When a linker must build an executable module from multiple object modules, it will commonly have to resolve public and external references. This is best understood by considering an example in which a call to a certain function exists within a program's main module but the declaration of that function is made within a separate module.

Listing 2.1 presents three different source code components of a program. Each of these components exists within a separate file with the first, WDEF.H, being a header file that is referenced within each of the other two files through an include statement. (For a full explanation of this book's use of pseudocode and action charts, see Appendix A.)

In this listing, the function main() will be compiled to an object module named MAIN.OBJ. A representation of this object module is shown in Figure 2.7. Only a few records are shown for the sake of simplicity. Note especially how the source statement extrn count_widgets() causes an EXTDEF record to be included in the object module. This is a signal telling the linker that the function count_widgets() must be found in some other object module.

The third section of Listing 2.1 shows the source code for count_widgets(). This source would compile into the CW.OBJ object module, a simplified model of which is shown in Figure 2.8. This module contains a PUBDEF record to tell the linker that the count_widgets() function resides within.

The file CW.OBJ could be specified to the linker as a separate standalone object module, or it could be placed within a library and specified to the linker in that manner. In the first sample link line below, CW.OBJ exists as a standalone module. In the second, CW.OBJ has been placed within the library file WIDGTLIB.LIB. The syntax in this example assumes the syntax of Microsoft's LINK.EXE product.

```
link main + cw;
link main,,,widgtlib;
```

As mentioned in the previous section, even though a library may contain hundreds of object modules, only those actually referenced will be linked into the final executable module. The story is different, however, when a list of standalone object modules is specified. All explicitly specified object modules are linked, regardless of whether any references are made to the code and data they contain.

```
┌─ struct w_data
│
│  byte count
│  w_data  *next
└─
```

---- Data definitions in the header file WDEF.H

```
include wdef.h

extrn count_widgets()

┌─ word main ()
│
│  w_data *widget_root
│  word total_widgets
│
│  allocate memory for widget data
│  read widget file into memory, building linked list
│   at widget_root
│  total_widgets = count_widgets(widget_root)
│  display value of total_widgets
│  return(0)
└─
```

---- Main program file, which forms MAIN.OBJ

```
include wdef.h

┌─ word count_widgets(w_data  *w-ptr)
│
│  word tally
│
│  ┌═ while(w_ptr  !=  NULL)
│  │  tally += w_ptr->count
│  │  w_ptr = w_ptr->next
│  └─
│
│  return (tally)
└─
```

---- Auxiliary program file, which forms CW.OBJ

LISTING 2.1 Example of EXTDEF and PUBDEF record usage

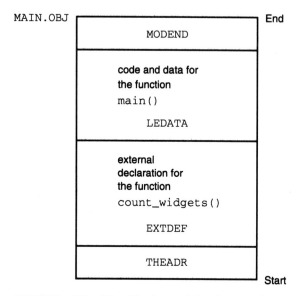

FIGURE 2.7 Simplified model of the object module MAIN.OBJ.

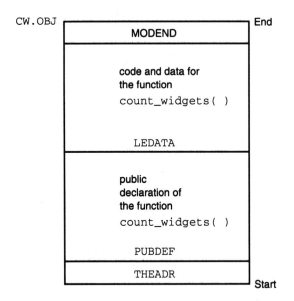

FIGURE 2.8 Simplified model of the object module CW.OBJ.

To resolve references, the linker first searches explicitly specified object modules and then searches the object modules within specified libraries. It is therefore possible to supersede functions normally obtained from a library module by using a standalone object module that contains functions by the same name. This approach can be useful when building a debugging version of a program.

During the linking process, a certain type of chain reaction is common. Say, for instance, that the object module MAIN.OBJ contains an external reference to a function named abc() (made through an EXTDEF record). When the linker finds function abc() within one of the specified libraries, it discovers an external reference to function def(). Another search of the library locates this function but also reveals an external reference within it for function ghi(). The linker must continue tracking such inter-module references until all have been resolved.

The first module specified to a linker plays a special role in two ways. First, the order of the code and data segments within this parent module defines the order that will be used in the final executable module. If the segmentation order of additional object modules differs from that of the first module, the linker will simply process the additional modules in such a way that they are made to conform to the template established by the first module. This control of order is important when working with the TSR and device driver program forms where resident and nonresident sections exist.

The first object module is also expected to contain the code that will form the program's initial entry point. When a program is loaded into memory for execution, the operating system will branch to this defined entry point, passing execution control of the computer to the program. This entry point must be defined within the first object module for the linker to build a proper binary module.

When a high-level language (HLL) compiler is used to build a program, more initial setup processing is often required than is accomplished by the very first statement in the program's main function. Most compiler packages deal with this by using a startup object module. This detail was neglected in Figure 2.5 for the sake of simplicity. Figure 2.9 rectifies this situation by showing how a startup module would be used.

INTRODUCTION TO LINK ORDER CONTROL

When it comes to building a program from separate object modules, there are three fundamental truths. Unfortunately, they are not entirely compatible.

1. Placing commonly used object modules within a library makes working with them much more convenient.

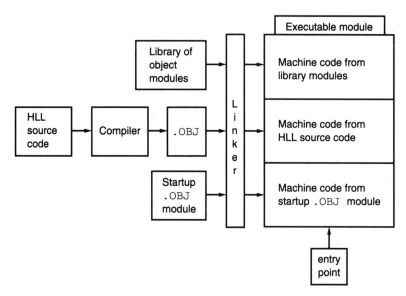

FIGURE 2.9 Linking in a startup object module.

2. When building a device driver or TSR, link-order control of the sections of the program is important. All parts of the program that will remain resident must be located within the first part of the final executable module, and all nonresident initialization code must be positioned at the end.
3. No direct means exists to control the link order of library modules.

When individual .OBJ modules are specified to the linker utility, it is possible to control the link order of the sections of the code represented by these modules. In simple terms, the contents of the first object module listed as an input to the linker will occupy the first position in the final output file, the second object module's contents will come next, and so on, until all have been accounted for.

However, when a library file (typically carrying the .LIB extension) is listed as a source of input to the linker utility, there is no simple way to control the position that the linker will assign to the contents of each object module pulled from that library module.

Certain link order control techniques must be employed when a program of the TSR or device driver form is to be built in which portions of the final binary module will come from a static link library. To understand the meaning of link order control, let's start by considering what happens when this aspect of the linking process is neglected. This should be pretty easy considering that it has yet to be defined!

In a simple library scheme where no special measures are taken, functions pulled in from libraries will be placed at the end of the executable module. This can be seen in Figure 2.9.

When a TSR or device driver involving resident and nonresident sections is being built, and if library functions are referenced from within the resident section but are placed at the end of the binary module, a dangerous situation is created. When the binary module is loaded and the nonresident section terminates with its report of how much memory should remain loaded, the module will "give away" the library functions. When the code in the resident section gains control and makes calls to the point in memory where those resident functions used to be, a crash is almost guaranteed.

Figure 2.10 illustrates the assembly and linking process for a TSR. For a device driver, the only difference would be in the nature of the entry point—the assembly and linking process would be no different. Figure 2.11 shows how a linker, when allowed to operate in its default manner, will append all library functions to the end of the final binary module.

The goal of the link order control technique is to support the use of static link libraries such that any library functions referenced from within the resident section are appended to the end of the resident section and any library functions referenced from within the nonresident section are placed at the end of that section. (See Figure 2.12.)

By properly accounting for link order control, it is possible to design libraries that will respond properly when called upon to build not only applications programs and standalone utility programs but TSRs and device drivers as well. This is accomplished through a coordinated system of program source templates, library module source templates, function-naming tricks, and segmentation-naming controls.

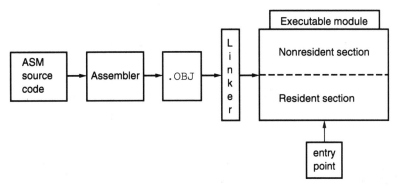

FIGURE 2.10 The compile and link process for a TSR.

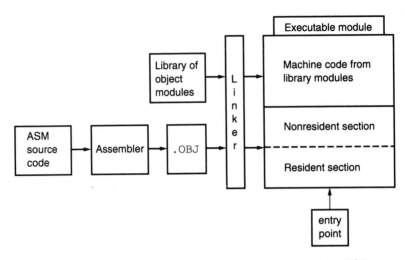

FIGURE 2.11 Involving a library in the construction of a TSR.

The basic idea is to have two different versions of each object module inserted into a library where the matching functions within each module have unique names. Naming-translation macros are then employed so that the programmer need only use one "normal" name for each function. If a reference to a library function occurs from within the nonresident section, these naming control macros automatically manipulate the ultimate name that the linker is

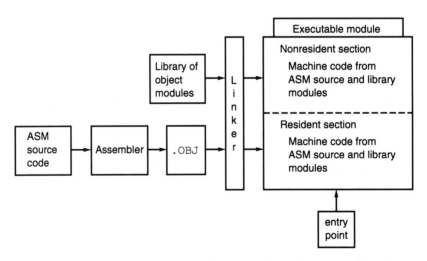

FIGURE 2.12 Link order control with a TSR.

made to see so that the non-resident library module is used. Likewise, when a library function is referenced from within the resident section, the macros change the name so that the linker pulls out the proper module for that section.

This technique will be covered in more detail from the tool-design perspective in Chapter 4, and from the library-design perspective in Chapter 5.

CHAPTER 3
Language Issues

The goal of this chapter is to familiarize you with the basic components of a program and the reasons for coding in a high-level language, in assembler, or in a mixture of each.

SINGLE-LANGUAGE PROGRAMS

Figure 3.1 illustrates a basic model of the processes involved in building a high-level language (HLL) program. For simplicity, this model ignores the details of data and stack segment creation. The intent is to show where the different program components come from and the processes involved in fusing them together into a meaningful whole. As you can see, the linker is the central controller in this operation.

The term "standard library" refers to the functions included as a standard part of the language package. In Pascal, for instance, this would include the code for functions such as `readln()`, `writeln()`, `assign()`, and `rewrite()`. In C, functions such as `printf()` and `atoi()` fall into this category.

Figure 3.2 shows how the basic process model of Figure 3.1 would be modified for a larger program where multiple source code modules are used. In a real-world program, there could actually be dozens, if not hundreds, of separate source files.

Another variation on this basic model is that with some language systems the compiler, linker, and startup module may be combined into one program.

Figure 3.3 presents a basic model for building an assembler (ASM) program. As above, this model ignores the details of data and stack segment

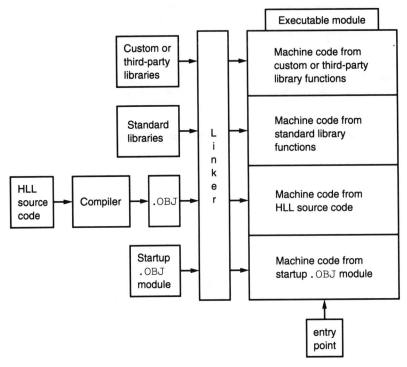

FIGURE 3.1   Composition of a typical HLL program.

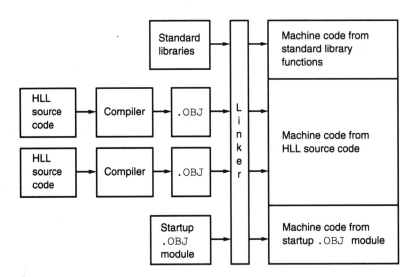

FIGURE 3.2   Separate compilation of multiple HLL source code modules.

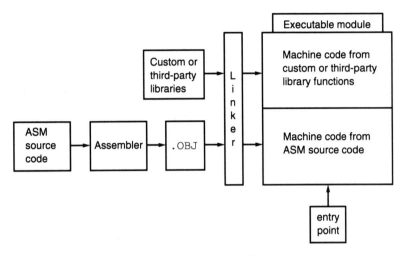

FIGURE 3.3 Composition of a typical ASM program.

creation. Also, as with the HLL case, more than one ASM source module could be involved in the build operation.

Note that while you can certainly use libraries with ASM, no Standard Library exists. Without libraries of some type, working with ASM means starting from scratch each time.

Developing in an HLL is typically more convenient than in ASM. This translates into less development time. Porting an HLL program to another compiler, operating system, or hardware platform is also typically much easier than with ASM. Further, while there's basically only one type of ASM per processor type, a plethora of HLL types exists, ranging from BASIC to C to specialized 4GL database languages. Finally, a larger selection of third-party function libraries is available for popular HLLs.

The HLL-only approach is not all roses, however. Some of the disadvantages include larger object code size and slower execution than are possible with ASM, as well as more limited control over processing action and code and data positioning.

Consequently, the HLL-only approach is not practical for developing a program of the TSR or device driver type. Yes, some do take this approach, but only by compromising on the efficient use of system memory. This is because it's not possible to separate initialization code and data cleanly from the code and data that must remain resident. A better solution for TSR and device driver construction is outlined below.

The ASM-only approach counters each of the disadvantages. Lean code sizing and fast execution are the hallmarks of the ASM program. It is also possible to exert a significant degree of control over the processing actions performed and over the organization of the code and data in memory. ASM is a natural for building TSRs and device drivers, as well as stand-alone utilities and full-scale applications packages.

A disadvantage of the ASM-only method is that it is more complicated than the HLL-only approach, there being many more details per unit of functionality. This detail management factor can extort a price in terms of longer initial development times and increased time requirements for debugging and ongoing maintenance. Other disadvantages include fewer ready-made function libraries, more difficulty in porting, and a more limited number of language development packages from which to choose.

MIXING ASM FUNCTIONS WITH AN HLL BASE

When you want or need some of the features of both approaches, it is possible to use a mixed model. Figure 3.4 outlines the construction of an HLL program where some of the functions are written in ASM. Since the HLL startup module is used, it is safe to use any of the HLL standard library functions.

This HLL/ASM technique (where HLL/ASM implies an HLL base) gives you more control over processing for selected parts of the program. It can also help reduce program size, to some extent, over the HLL-only approach. One of the most common reasons for employing this method, however, is to reduce the execution time of the functions that have a high rate of execution—bottleneck functions.

While most HLL packages do support the generation of software interrupt calls, interrupt-handling functions, and reading and writing absolute memory locations and I/O ports, the resulting machine code is never as lean and fast as when such functions are written directly in ASM. There are also cases where an interrupt handler will need to switch to a local stack. Try doing that with an HLL!

As with the HLL-only and ASM-only cases already described, it is possible to compile or assemble multiple source modules and have the linker merge all the corresponding .OBJ files into the final executable module.

Many compilers sport a feature known as *in-line assembly*. When used, the process is basically the same as that pictured in Figure 3.4. The only difference is that the compiler extracts the in-line assembly instructions from the HLL source file, writes them to a temporary .ASM file, and spawns an assembler to produce the object module (an .OBJ file). Some compilers may also support a built-in assembler, which eliminates the need to write a temporary source file and spawn an external assembler program, but the net effect is still the same.

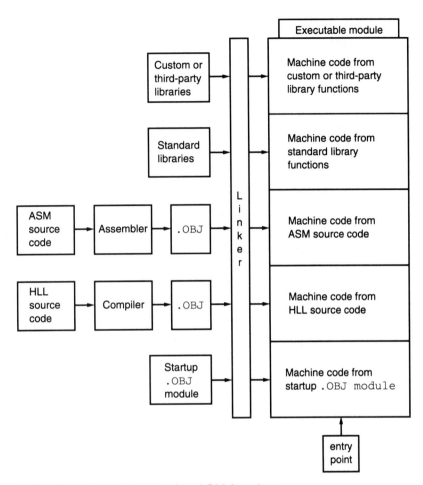

FIGURE 3.4 HLL base using ASM functions.

If your goal is to construct a TSR or device driver, the HLL/ASM mixture is still not the best answer. The use of the startup object module that comes with the HLL package limits your control over the organization of the code and data within the binary load module.

When it comes to the design and coding of the ASM portion, there are two different avenues you can take: write the ASM functions directly in assembler language in the first place, or write a first draft of them in HLL and then convert.

If not precluded by the very limitations of HLL that you must circumvent, you can start by writing a preliminary HLL version of your logic. Keep in mind that it will run more slowly and occupy more memory than the eventual ASM version. Once this version has passed initial testing, make your compiler output an ASM source file and study and optimize the code. By modifying this code to use registers instead of stack-based local variables and by eliminating redundant loading of pointers, you can often achieve an acceptable performance increase.

Limitations do exist, however. No matter how efficient your optimizations, if the underlying algorithm is mediocre, the final product's performance will be hampered by that fact. In such cases, it is better to design in ASM from the start.

As an example of this type of hindering, consider the case of a program that must perform repeated searches through an unordered array of records using one of the record's fields as the search key. Starting with HLL logic, a typical algorithm would be to access each record in the array sequentially within a loop, testing for a match between the key field and the search key. (For the sake of this example, assume that the search key is an unsigned 16-bit integer type.)

To achieve the fastest execution speed, redesign the logic to take advantage of the assembler SCASW string search instruction in combination with the REPNE repeat prefix. Note that this will require the key fields for each record to be located within one contiguous list within memory. This can be accomplished either by building a transitory list of index keys, where data redundancy is accepted, or by reorganizing the array into two parallel arrays—one for the key field and another for the remaining fields.

MIXING HLL FUNCTIONS WITH AN ASM BASE

Figure 3.5 presents the basic model for a program comprised of an ASM substrate where HLL functions can be used. This arrangement is well suited for the construction of TSRs and device drivers where the convenience of HLL development is desired but the precise control of ASM is also necessary. In system-level drivers of this type, HLL code is a practical choice for initialization code such as parameter-parsing logic, where size and speed are not critical concerns. Of course, you can also use HLL code for the resident logic when size and speed requirements don't mandate ASM code.

For this approach to succeed, the HLL compiler must be able to produce a "pure" object module. A compiler/linker package that can only produce a stand-alone .EXE file would not work. Neither would a compiler whose object modules all require the inclusion of the standard startup module.

Note that the exclusion of the standard HLL startup module has both good and bad points. The benefit is that your ASM startup module can be designed to control code placement and to initialize global variables and

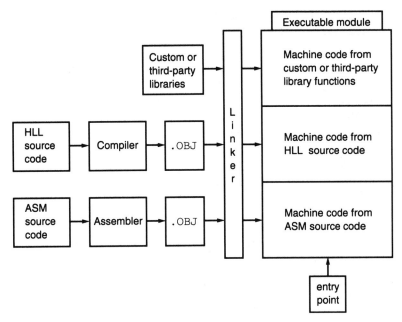

FIGURE 3.5 ASM base using HLL functions.

common logic (such as error handlers) as your needs dictate. The downside is that while HLL modules may be used, it is not safe to use standard library functions unless you have a thorough knowledge of their implementation.

In many cases, these library functions will count on certain initialization operations having been done by the standard HLL startup module. Even if you do have the source code for your compiler's library and do determine that certain functions can be used, you must then always purchase this source with each compiler upgrade, keep track of which functions you are counting on being independent, and reverify their independence in each new release.

SUMMARY OF LANGUAGE MODELS

This book's Companion Diskette contains templates for creating each of the just-described program types in assembler and C. Table 3.1 summarizes the advantages and disadvantages of the various construction techniques.

TABLE 3.1   Features of various construction techniques

	HLL Alone	ASM Alone	ASM Base HLL/ASM Funcs	HLL Base HLL/ASM Funcs
Control of processing actions	Limited	Almost unlimited	Almost unlimited	Almost unlimited
Control of code positioning	Limited	Almost unlimited	Almost unlimited	Almost unlimited
Suitability for TSR or Device Driver	Poor	Good	Good	Poor
Execution speed	Slow to moderate	Fast	Moderate to fast	Moderate to fast
Bytes of code per operation	High	Low	Moderate	Moderate
Readability	Good	Poor	Mixed	Mixed
Ease of use	Good	Poor	Mixed	Mixed
Safe to use standard library functions	Yes	N/A	Sometimes	Yes

CHAPTER 4
Building Tools

Much of this chapter is concerned with the application of templates in software tool development. Templates are included for the construction of stand-alone ASM and C programs, but there is nothing critical about their design. If you are only concerned with building HLL stand-alone programs, most of this chapter's text doesn't apply. In the next chapter, pay particular attention to the section on stripping the link order control operations out of the library building process.

When you intend to build TSRs or device drivers that can take advantage of library functions through the link order control scheme, the provided templates will prove invaluable.

THE TEMPLATE FILES

The Companion Diskette contains the following source code template files to handle the most common tool-building situations. These files are located within the \ZLIB\WORK\STOCK directory:

STANDA.ASM	Template for a stand-alone ASM program
STANDC.C	Template for a stand-alone C program
TSR.ASM	Template for a TSR
DDSTRTUP.ASM	Startup code for device drivers
DDSTOCK.MAK	Make file for device drivers
DDRSTOCK.C	Template for device driver, resident portion

```
DDTSTOCK.C        Template for device driver, nonresident portion
DDHSTOCK.INC      Template for device driver, header
```

The STANDA.ASM template is designed to produce a stand-alone program from assembler source code. An executable binary file of the .EXE type is the intended result.

The STANDC.C template produces a stand-alone program from C source code. An executable binary file of the .EXE type is the likely result (depending on your chosen C compiler). Since this module will contain the compiler's startup code, Standard C Library functions may be used. In addition, ASM code modules could be assembled into separate .OBJ modules and linked in with this module.

The TSR.ASM template is designed to produce a TSR program from assembler source code. An executable binary file of the .EXE type is the intended result. C code modules could be compiled into separate .OBJ modules and linked in with this module (see the discussion of the MODOBJ.EXE utility later in this chapter). Library functions from the Standard C Library should not be used, since the compiler's startup code is not included in the linking process. Since this template has been designed to work in concert with the link order control scheme, any conforming library functions may be used.

The remaining five files in the foregoing list are involved in the creation of device drivers. As will be explained below, this device driver construction method supports drivers composed of all ASM code or of a mixture of ASM and C (or any other conforming HLL). While Standard C Library functions are again off-limits, library functions that conform to the link order control scheme can be used.

An executable binary file of the .EXE type is the intended result (though a .SYS extension is used to prevent confusion with stand-alone and TSR programs).

GETSTOCK.BATM and Other Batch Files

The process of making working copies of the template files is simplified through the use of the GETSTOCK.BAT batch file. This file is located within the \ZLIB\BATCH directory. It requires two parameters. The first must be one of the terms in the following list:

```
STANDA      (to copy the STANDA.ASM template)
STANDC      (to copy the STANDC.C template)
TSR         (to copy the TSR.ASM template)
SYS         (to copy the device driver templates)
```

The second parameter must be the name that is to be used for your new source code module. For example, when you want to build a TSR named WATCHER, use GETSTOCK as follows, and you will end up with a copy of the TSR.ASM template named WATCHER.ASM:

```
getstock tsr watcher
```

When you need to build a stand-alone C program named EATFILES, use GETSTOCK as follows and the file EATFILES.C will result. The case for a stand-alone assembler program is similar.

```
getstock standc eatfiles
```

The remaining use of GETSTOCK is in preparing a set of source files for a device driver. Each device driver built by this book's method is composed of a set of files. Three files—two .C modules and one .INC (assembler include) module—are unique to each driver. There are two additional files that are common to all drivers: \ZLIB\WORK\STOCK\DDSTRTUP.ASM and \ZLIB\WORK\STOCK\DDSTOCK.MAK.

To use GETSTOCK to generate a set of the three unique files, you must use sys as the first parameter and the base filename of your driver as the second parameter. This base name must be a valid filename and must be no longer than seven characters. When this device driver construction method produces the ultimate binary module, the filename used will be your specified base filename.

As an example, entering the GETSTOCK command as follows would produce the listed set of files:

```
getstock sys ramdisk
```

RAMDISK.DDH	The device driver's head
RAMDISKR.C	Source code for the driver's resident section
RAMDISKT.C	Source code for the driver's nonresident section

The ultimate binary module produced from this set of files would be named RAMDISK.SYS. Note how the filenames of the two .C modules have had an additional character appended. The T, for "transient," denotes the source file that is to contain the nonresident code and data. The R denotes the source module that is to contain the resident code and data. The need to append this additional character is why the base name must be limited to seven characters.

It is also possible to use this construction method to build a driver composed entirely of ASM code or to adapt it to other conforming HLL situations. More on this will be shown later in this chapter.

The following set of batch files is provided to simplify the process of building programs based on this book's templates. They are located in the \ZLIB\BATCH directory of the companion diskette.

MDD.BAT	Produces a .SYS device driver file based on the DD*.* set of templates
ME.BAT	Produces an .EXE file from an .ASM file
CLC.BAT	Produces an .EXE file from a .C file

The MDD.BAT batch file is designed to process a set of device driver files and produce a binary module of the .SYS type. It invokes your MAKE program with the \ZLIB\WORK\STOCK\DDSTOCK.MAK makefile, passing the driver's base filename in through the -Dbase parameter.

The function of the ME.BAT batch file is to produce an .EXE file from an assembler source code module. The name ME stands for Make Exe. It would be used with files derived from the STANDA.ASM and TSR.ASM templates. At minimum, one parameter is expected: the filename of the .ASM module to process. If d is specified as a second parameter, debugging information will be produced during the assembly and linking process (for use with a source-level or symbolic debugger).

The CLC.BAT (for Command-Line Compiler) batch file is designed to be used with files copied from the STANDC.C template. The parameter conventions for this batch file are the same as for ME.BAT.

LINK ORDER CONTROL FOR TOOLS

If you'll recall from the discussion in Chapter 2, the link order control scheme is what makes it possible for two-part software entities, such as TSRs and device drivers, to make use of library functions. Without this linkage control technique, functions needed by the resident section of a tool would end up linked after the end-of-resident point.

From the tool-building perspective, support for link order control involves a combination of three techniques:

1. The use of multiple code and data segments within all programs to be developed under this library method. The resident code and data segments (one code, two data) are given the names RTEXT, RDATA,

and RBSS, with the corresponding nonresident segments given the names _TEXT, _DATA, and _BSS.

2. The use of macros that modify the names ultimately used for library functions, so that the final name depends on whether the reference is made from within the resident or nonresident section.

3. The existence of two copies of each library function within the .LIB file. The segment names and function name of one copy have been modified for the resident case, and the other copy is set for the nonresident case.

The full range of peculiarities involved in multisegment linking is beyond the scope of this book. For more details on these peculiarities, consult the user's manual for the linker portion of your chosen compiler or assembler. For the sake of this discussion, please accept the following summary.

To get an idea of the linking process involved when multiple code and data segments are being used within multiple object modules, it can be helpful to think of a game of cards. In this game, there are two players, a dealer, a playing table, and, of course, a deck of cards. Player #1 is the resident section of the final program, with player #2 being the nonresident section. The dealer, in this analogy, is the linker, and the playing table represents the code and data from the main source code module of the program being constructed (the template). Last, but not least, the deck of cards represents the function library.

The dealer (the linker) begins by picking up the freshly shuffled deck of cards (the function library—"shuffled" because the functions may be located in any order within the .LIB file). The dealer then inspects a wish list that player #1 has presented and searches through the deck for the cards in that list, placing those found in a stack on the playing table in front of player #1. After that, it's player #2's turn to present its wish list and have its stack built.

When the dealing is finished, what you have is a playing table with two neatly ordered stacks of cards on it. Viewing the table and card stacks as their real-life counterparts, you now have a properly formed program where functions have been pulled in from a library file and located in the correct portion of the final executable module.

The dealer orders the stacks correctly because the name-modifying macros and multiple-segment configuration force it to. When the dealer doesn't have benefit of the extra information made possible through this method, the entire set of cards (library functions) in the wish lists of both players is placed in one stack on player #2's side of the table (the nonresident section of the program).

In the assembler case, the lcall macro is responsible for the function name manipulations. While this method is transparent to the programmer for the most part, a small concession is necessary on the part of a programmer using this tool construction system. Any call made to a function within the Companion Diskette's function library must be made using the `lcall` macro instead of the normal `call` instruction.

In the following example piece of code, the nonlibrary function named `local_function` is called using the normal `call` instruction, but the `la_word2hex` function is located within the Companion Library and must therefore be referenced using the `lcall` macro. Actually, this can be thought of as a form of documentation, since it provides anyone reading this source code with a useful bit of information—the location of the called function.

```
mov     ax,[widget_class]
call    local_function
mov     bx,[total_widgets]
mov     si,offset dgroup:buffer
lcall   la_word2hex
```

The `lcall` macro, located within the file `\ZLIB\LA_MACS.INC`, works in conjunction with an assembler `SET` variable named `reslib`. This `SET` variable must be assigned the value of 1 at the start of the resident section of the main program's source code module and then reassigned the value of 0 at the start of the nonresident section. This detail has already been taken care of in this book's templates.

When the `SET` variable `reslib` holds a value of 0, this macro produces a `call` instruction in which a `t` (for "transient") is appended to the end of the specified library function's name for the nonresident case. When `reslib` holds the value of 1, an `r` (for "resident") is appended to the specified function name. In either case, an underscore character is prepended to the specified name. This is done for compatibility with the C language's function-naming convention.

Thus, even though you code an `lcall` statement to a function named `la_word2hex`, there is actually no library function with that exact name. Rather, there are two library functions: one named `_la_word2hexr` and another named `_la_word2hext`. In addition, the resident version, `_la_word2hexr`, is coded within a module using the `RTEXT`, `RDATA`, and `RBSS` segments. Likewise, the `_la_word2hext` function is coded to use the `_TEXT`, `_DATA`, and `_BSS` segments. To revisit the card game analogy briefly, the name manipulation causes the dealer to find the right card for the wish list being processed, and the corresponding segment names make sure that the dealer places the card in the right stack.

Note that when a stand-alone assembler program is being developed, in which there are no resident and nonresident sections, you still must use the `lcall` macro. Fortunately for you, by using this macro you can remain largely oblivious to this naming manipulation.

One further detail which must be attended to when functions are used from the Companion Library, is that a special macro must be used when the function is declared as external. This macro is named `lextrn` and is also located within the file `\ZLIB\LA_MACS.INC`. With a normal `extrn` statement you must supply an ending term, such as `near`, but with `lextrn` this is not necessary.

```
reslib = 1
lextrn la_word2hex
```

Were you to inspect the actual expansion text for the foregoing use of this macro, here is what you would see:

```
extrn _la_word2hexr:near
```

In the C case, due to the nature of its macro preprocessor, life with this library technique is even simpler. To use a function from the library requires nothing special; all you have to do is reference the function in the normal manner. For example, to use the `lc_word2hex()` function to convert a word value to its hexadecimal representation within a text buffer:

```
lc_word2hex ( &buffer[5], total_widgets );
```

As long as the header file `\ZLIB\ZLIBDEFS.H` is included within your program (as it is in the program templates), the naming manipulation will be taken care of in a transparent manner. The macros within this header file manipulate the function name based on the current value of the `#defined` variable `reslib`, just as in the assembler case.

RESIDENT/NONRESIDENT PROGRAMMING

When working with the TSR and device driver templates, it is important to realize that the initialization code within the `_TEXT` segment uses a different value in the CS register from that used by the resident code within the `RTEXT` segment. Any and all intersegment calls must, therefore, be far calls.

A pair of macros is provided to simplify this situation in the ASM case. These macros, named `lcall` and `lgpcall`, are found in the `\ZLIB\LA_MACS.INC` include file.

The `lcall` macro observes the following rules:

- If `lcall` is used within the resident section, it will form a call to the resident version of a library function (where an underscore is prepended and an r is appended). The function can be either near or far.

- If lcall is used within the nonresident section and the library function being called is defined within the resident section, a proper call instruction will be generated only if the function is declared as a far function (for example, by using the proc far keywords).

- If lcall is used within the nonresident section and the library function being called is defined within the nonresident section, then the function can either be near or far.

The second macro, lgpcall, is intended for the specific case where a library function is of the near type, is located within the resident section, but must be called from one or more points within the nonresident section. The lgpcall macro solicits the aid of a library function named la_gpcsh (General-Purpose Calling SHell).

This calling shell performs the necessary stack manipulations to make an intersegment call to a near function possible. The only drawback is that this calling shell cannot be used with functions that rely on stack parameters or with functions that switch stacks (such as the la_local_context and la_orig_context functions, which are discussed subsequently).

When it comes to an HLL such as C, most functions do involve stack-based parameters, so a calling shell is not possible. If the ultimate function you need to call is near, you will have to make a dedicated calling shell function of your own.

In the following example, the actual need was for the resident function xyz() to be called from a point within the nonresident module. To accomplish this, a new function, XYZ_F(), had to be created within the resident section:

- In the resident C module:

```
byte far xyz_f ( byte t )
{

    return ( xyz ( t ) );
}
```

- In the nonresident C module:

```
extern far byte xyz_f ( byte t );

tt = xyz_f ( 3 );
```

Even though the resident and nonresident code segments are different, they both use the same segment for data and stack access. As a result, it is possible to declare a variable within the resident C module, write an `extern` for it in the nonresident C module, and then have the nonresident code access that data. Doing the opposite, however, would not be wise. It would compile and link without problems, but once the tool is installed, its nonresident code and data are no longer in memory. The resident code would be addressing a memory location that would have already been put to a different use.

STACK ISSUES

Since the development of device drivers and TSR-type utilities is a central theme in this chapter, this is a good time to study some issues relating to stack usage. Software constructs, such as interrupt handlers, and mixed language models tend to involve system-level programming, including stack switching, stack addressing, and reentrance.

The goal is to develop one common set of library functions that will handle stack-switching needs in general.

Stack Addressing with the BP Register

The most basic rule to remember is that any time the SP register is loaded into the BP register, the SS:BP pointer points to what was last pushed onto the stack at the time BP was loaded with SP. (The use of the BP register automatically implies the use of the SS segment register, unless an explicit segment override is given.) From there, an offset of +2 would be used to access each higher word on the stack. Here are some examples:

```
push    ax
push    bx
push    cx
push    bp
mov     bp,sp
mov     ax,[bp]          ; access original bp
mov     ax,[bp+2]        ; access original cx
mov     ax,[bp+4]        ; access original bx
mov     ax,[bp+6]        ; access original ax

push    bp
push    ax
push    bx
```

```
sub     sp,4                ; create 2 words of local
                            ; storage
mov     bp,sp
mov     word ptr [bp],123   ; write to lower
                            ; local word
mov     word ptr [bp+2],456 ; write to higher
                            ; local word
mov     ax,[bp+4]           ; access original bx
mov     ax,[bp+6]           ; access original ax
mov     ax,[bp+8]           ; access original bp
```

Often, local stack-based storage will be allocated after the BP register is loaded from SP. This results in the use of negative offsets, as shown in the following example:

```
push    bp
mov     bp,sp
sub     sp,10               ; create a 5 word local
                            ; pocket
mov     [bp-2],ax           ; use highest word
mov     [bp-4],bx           ; use next word
mov     [bp-6],cx           ; etc.
mov     [bp-8],dx
mov     [bp-10],si          ; use lowest word
```

Given the stack frame laid in place by this code fragment, here are some examples of byte-level access to stack frame data:

```
; does entry ah == 3c?

        cmp     byte ptr [bp-1],03ch
        je      is_3c

; change stack copy of bl to 2

        mov     byte ptr [bp-4],2
```

Finally, as you'll see if you inspect the assembler code produced by a high-level language compiler such as C, positive-offset BP addressing is used to access stack-based entry parameters, while negative-offset BP addressing is used to access local stack variables.

The following code fragment shows two functions within a small-model C program and the corresponding assembler code. Here is the pair of C functions:

```
void process_widgets ( int parameter_var )
{

  int local_var;

  local_var = parameter_var;
}

void main()
{

  process_widgets ( 44 );
}
```

Following is the equivalent assembler code:

```
_process_widgets proc near
        push    bp
        mov     bp,sp
        dec     sp
        dec     sp
        mov     ax,word ptr [bp+4]
        mov     word ptr [bp-2],ax
        mov     sp,bp
        pop     bp
        ret
_process_widgets endp

_main proc near
        push    bp
        mov     bp,sp
        mov     ax,44
        push    ax
        call    near ptr _process_widgets
        pop     cx
        pop     bp
        ret
_main endp
```

In the foregoing C code, the variable local_var is declared within the process_widgets() function without the static modifier. This makes it a stack-based automatic variable. Within the assembler version, the purpose of two dec sp instructions is to allocate a word of local stack storage for this variable. So, what a C programmer knows as `local_var` would now be known to an assembler programmer as `word ptr [bp-2]`.

Now let's take a look at how C passes the entry parameter value of 44 into the `process_widgets()` function (the literal value 44 is used when this function is called from within `main()`). In the assembler code version of `main()`, note how the literal value of 44 is loaded into the AX register and then pushed onto the stack. The stack word is the actual entry parameter to the `process_widgets` function. The fact that this data is also within the AX register is purely coincidental.

Within `process_widgets()`, this stack-based entry parameter is accessed through the `word ptr [bp+4]` operand. The offset of +4 is used to account for the near return address placed on the stack by the `call` instruction. Here is how the stack is arranged once the stack setup epilogue of `_process_widgets` has been executed (when the current instruction would be the `mov ax,word ptr [bp+4]`):

bp+4	the data passed in for `parameter_var`
bp+2	the near return address
bp+0	the entry BP value
bp-2	storage for the `local_var` variable

Stack Switching

One of the most common situations where stack switching must be employed is in the coding of interrupt intercepts. In the most basic sense, all that is required is that the current values within the SS:SP register pair be saved somewhere and that new values be assigned. This would, of course, be done right at the start of an intercept handler, with a corresponding restoration of the previous SS:SP values done at the end. But, as you may have surmised from skimming ahead and noting the size of this section, there's a little more involved than this "most basic" idea.

A PC/AT-type machine is designed to make use of a number of hardware interrupts. Approximately 18 times per second, the 8253 timer asserts an IRQ0 interrupt, causing the `INT08` handler to gain control. Every time you press or release a key, an IRQ1 interrupt occurs (vectored to `INT09`). In addition, IRQ-type interrupts are caused by disk drives, mice, video display adapters, and a number of other peripherals. The `NMI` type (Non-Maskable Interrupt) must also be included in this category.

Whenever it is possible for a hardware interrupt to occur, a valid stack must exist on which the return address and current flags values can be placed. Most interrupt handlers will also require stack space to save the original values the general-purpose CPU registers that must be used by the handler. This same consideration applies equally to intercepts that are established on hardware interrupts.

Since two registers are involved, SS and SP, establishing a new stack means that two instructions must be executed (actually, the 80386 CPU did introduce an `lss sp,[memvar]` instruction). If it were possible for an interrupt to occur in between these two instructions, the memory used for the stack by that interrupt would not be a proper stack. It would be whatever memory was pointed to by the transitional SS:SP stack pointer value, where one of the registers held a new value and the other still held an old value.

To make sure that the process of loading SS and SP is secure against any type of interrupt, including NMI, the 80×86 type of CPU was designed so that loading a new value into the SS register automatically makes the next instruction immune from interruption. The intention, of course, is that this next instruction be the one that loads the SP register with its new value. For example:

```
mov     ss,[newss]
mov     sp,[newsp]
```

Occasionally, you'll find a program whose designers felt they needed to perform additional operations in between the loading of SS and SP. Realizing that switching stacks was a sensitive operation, they attempt to guard the stack switch from interruption by disabling interrupts:

```
cli
mov     ss,[newss]
sub     [newsp],stk_bias
mov     sp,[newsp]
sti
```

This method will prevent problems with the normal type of hardware interrupt, but if an NMI interrupt should occur in between the `sub [newsp],stk_bias` instruction and the `mov sp,[newsp]` instruction, the collective SS:SP value would be invalid and a crash would occur.

Given that the normal use of the NMI within a PC/AT system is to signal a memory parity error, this flaw may be of little consequence. But problems can also occur when this type of code is traced using a debugger's single-step feature. When you trace through the instruction that loads the SS register, the next instruction will automatically be skipped.

This will place you at the `mov sp,[newsp]` instruction—if you're lucky! When the CPU is single-stepping, an INT01 will automatically occur after each instruction. In this case, however, the stack used by the INT01 instruction will be half-baked. Whatever memory happens to be pointed to by the new SS and the old SP will be overwritten by the stack usage implicit in the execution of the INT01 interrupt.

The moral of this story is to keep your stack-switching code clean and safe. Always make use of the automatic interrupt-guarding feature provided when a new value is loaded into the SS register.

Now for the strange part. Even though you design your stack-switching code to work with the automatic guarding feature, you should also surround each stack switch with `cli` and `sti` instructions. There are reportedly some early versions of the 8088 CPU in existence that contain a flaw (a hardware bug) whereby this automatic stack guarding doesn't always work. Therefore, to avoid problems on older machines, here's the final recipe:

```
cli
mov     ss,[newss]
mov     sp,[newsp]
sti
```

A First-Cut Attempt

Listing 4.1 shows a first-cut attempt at incorporating stack-switching code into an intercept. Note that the prologue code does make use of the automatic interrupt-guarding technique, since the loading of a new SP value immediately follows the loading of a new SS value.

Where this first-cut attempt falls short is in its handling of reentrance. Interrupt handlers are notorious for being reentered. This is where the prologue portion of the handler is executed once for the original entry and is then executed again before the first entry is balanced with an exit. In other words, while the system is executing within an interrupt handler, some action occurs that causes another call to be made to that same interrupt. Consequently, any intercept logic you write should be designed to account for this possibility.

What would happen if the intercept handler within Listing 4.1 was reentered? First of all, the [savess] and [savesp] memory variables would be reused by the second entry before their values would serve their purpose to the first entry. When this nesting of calls would finally unwind to the point where the original entry was concluding, the stack restoration logic at the end of the intercept would end up using the SS:SP values saved upon the second entrance rather than the first.

If this isn't enough, all information placed on the local stack by the first entrance will be overwritten by the second entrance. This would occur because

```
i21_icept:
        mov     cs:[savess],ss  ; use cs:  override
        mov     cs:[savesp],sp  ; to access local data
        push    cs
        pop     ss
        mov     sp,offset top_of_lcl_stk
        sti

        .....
          (1st section of intercept logic)
        .....

        pushf
        cli
        call    cs:[i21_orig]
        pushf

        .....
          (2nd section of intercept logic)
        .....

        popf
        cli
        mov     ss,cs:[savess]
        mov     sp,cs:[savesp]
        retf    2
```

LISTING 4.1   Intercept stack switching (not stable, see text)

when a local stack is provided for the second entrance, the same stack offset is used as for the first entry.

So, we've got some problems here. Before attending to solutions, let's deal with the question: "How can reentrance occur in the first place?" It's always good to have a clear understanding of a problem before you set out to find its cure.

There are several ways that reentrance can occur. First of all, it can be due to an intentionally recursive type of call. In the INT10 video BIOS logic, function number 13h is provided to write a string of characters to the display. In some BIOS implementations, this function performs its task by itself making INT10 calls in which the AH function selector values are for lower-level functions, such as 09h (write character) and 02h (set new cursor position). If you set up an INT10 intercept and a call is made to function 13h, your intercept handler will be reentered due to the actions of these recursive calls.

Reentrance could also occur due to the actions of a previously installed intercept handler. Suppose you have a tool that is intercepting INT21 calls, and when your intercept logic makes its pass-on call, another INT21 intercept gains control. This handler could set a reentrance control flag and then issue INT21 calls as part of its intercept-processing activities. Even though this previously installed intercept has set a flag to let its own entrance logic know that a recursion will occur, your intercept will be reentered, but with no knowledge of this flag.

Making additional INT21 calls from an INT21 intercept is safe and is not uncommon in debugging tools, CD-ROM redirector drivers, and network redirectors. It is often done to get and set the current PSP (functions 50h and 51h) or to record details of the original INT21 call within a file. Note that a better way to make INT21 calls from within an INT21 intercept is to execute a pushf and cli and then make a far call to the previous INT21 vector, which your intercept driver will have already recorded.

Another way reentrance could occur involves those pop-up window–type TSR utilities, such as phone dialers and calculators. Such a utility could be hooked into the INT08 or INT1C timer interrupt, watching for an acceptable time to pop up by checking the INDOS flag. This timer interrupt could occur just after your intercept logic has switched to its local stack but before the INT21 call has been passed on to DOS. Therefore, the INDOS flag will be clear, and the TSR will pop up. When this utility issues its first INT21 call, your intercept logic will be reentered. Refer to books on constructing this type of utility for more details on the INDOS flag.

Interrupt handler reentrance can also occur with IRQ-type interrupts. It may be that the amount of time required to process certain interrupt events will be so long that another one of those same interrupts occurs before the previous one has completed. As long as this only happens occasionally and the code has been designed to expect it, there is nothing intrinsically wrong with this scenario.

Actually, the underlying issue is not reentrance into the same interrupt handler, but reuse of the same stack space. If you were to develop a tool with an INT21 intercept and an INT10 intercept, where the same local stack was switched to upon entry to each handler, you would be in trouble for the case where you intercept an INT21 call that happens to issue an INT10 call. The INT10 intercept would overwrite the stack information that the INT21 intercept is counting on.

A Better Way

The intercept shown in Listing 4.2 does not represent a complete solution, but it is a step in the right direction. In this version, the original SS:SP values

```
i21_icept:
        push    bx
        push    es
        mov     bx,ss
        mov     es,bx
        mov     bx,sp
        push    cs
        cli
        pop     ss
        mov     sp,offset top_of_lcl_stk
        push    es
        push    bx
        sti


        .....
          (1st section of intercept logic)
        .....

        pushf
        cli
        call    cs:[i21_orig]


        .....
          (2nd section of intercept logic)
        .....

        cli
        pop     bx
        pop     ss              ; pushed as es
        mov     sp,bx
        pop     es
        pop     bx
        iret
```

LISTING 4.2 Storing SS:SP on the stack (still not stable)

are stored within the ES:BX register pair. The contents of the ES:BX register pair is then saved on the new stack for the duration of the intercept.

While this version does store the entry SS:SP values in a way that is resilient to reentrance, the second problem noted above still remains. Should a reentrance occur, all data placed on the local stack by the first entrance will be overwritten by the second.

Another difference between this intercept method and the intercept handlers previously presented in this chapter is that the values of certain registers aren't directly accessible anymore. Extra steps would be required to fetch the entry values for the ES and BX registers before the interrupt call is passed on to the previous vector holder. In some interrupt intercept tools (such as debugging tools), it is also necessary to locate the CS:IP return address from the entry stack so that the location of the interrupt call can be determined and dumped to an output display. Note that after the stack switch, the ES:BX register pair does point to the caller's stack where these values are located.

Further, for the case of a software interrupt, after the pass-on call is made to the previous vector holder, the current values of the ES and BX registers and the CPU flags register must be transferred back to the original point of call. Since ES and BX must also be used to restore the original SS:SP values, some nontrivial cross-stack manipulations would be required to transplant the returning ES, BX, and flags values.

Regarding the problem with the reuse of the same area of the local stack, one idea would be to detect when a reentrant call is being made and use a lower point on the local stack. A method sometimes used to detect a reentrance is to test the value of the SS stack segment register upon entry to the intercept. If it is the same as that of the local stack, a reentrance is being made.

The problem with this method is that it isn't foolproof. The fact that a reentrance is possible means that some other software entity (such as an IRQ handler) has gained control during a time when your local stack was in effect. This other entity could have switched to its own local stack before making this call, preventing your test of the SS register from working properly.

Listing 4.3 shows a trio of functions and a data structure taken from this book's Companion Library. These functions are designed to support reentrance within interrupt intercepts and also provide easy access to the full set of entry registers without the problems just described.

These functions require that a variable named [ld_lstk] exist to hold the offset to be used for the local stack. Although not shown here, the actual library module from which these functions were taken includes both a declaration of this word-sized field and a function that would be used to assign the initial value to this field. For the sake of this discussion, assume that this memory variable has been seeded with the offset of the top of the local stack buffer. The library source code module that contains these functions is named \ZLIB\LIBSRC\CONTEXT.ASM.

The way these routines deal with the problems involved in local stack switching and reentrance is by throwing memory at them. There's actually nothing else you can do, unless you can prevent the reentrance in the first place or detect it early on and skip the processing of nested events.

```
regset struc
osp     dw      ?
oss     dw      ?
obp     dw      ?
oes     dw      ?
ods     dw      ?
odi     dw      ?
osi     dw      ?
odx     dw      ?
ocx     dw      ?
obx     dw      ?
oax     dw      ?
onret   dw      ?
oip     dw      ?
ocs     dw      ?
oflags  dw      ?
regset ends
```

```
;===================================================================
; la_local_context
;
; Switch to a local stack.
;
; NOTE: A call to la_setlstk must be made one time before
; la_local_context and la_orig_context can be used.
;
; Call la_adjlstk right after calling this function.
;
; In:    registers = interrupt calling registers
;        fl, cs and ip on stack from int call
;
; Out:   caller's registers in save area on caller's stack
;        es:bx -> register save area
;        ss:sp -> local stack
;        ds -> DGROUP
;        interrupts disabled (will be enabled by la_adjlstk)
;===================================================================
```

(continued on next page)

LISTING 4.3 Stack functions from the Companion Library

```
        assume  ds:nothing,es:nothing,ss:nothing
lname la_local_context
        push    ax
        push    bx
        push    cx
        push    dx
        push    si
        push    di
        push    ds
        push    es
        push    bp
        push    ss
        mov     ax,sp           ; can't just do a 'push sp,' since
        push    ax              ; its 8086 action != 80286+  action
        cli                     ; ensure interrupts are off
        mov     ax,ss
        mov     es,ax
        mov     bx,sp
        mov     ax,seg DGROUP
        mov     ds,ax
        assume  ds:DGROUP
        mov     ss,ax
        mov     sp,DGROUP:[ld_lstk]
        push    es:[bx].onret
        ret


;========================================================================
; la_adjlstk
;
; Adjust [ld_lstk] to prepare for possible reentry
;
; NOTE: A call to la_setlstk must be made one time before
; la_local_context and la_orig_context can be used.
;
; This function is to be called right after la_local_context.
;
; In:    ax = amount to be subtracted from ld_lstk
;        ds -> DGROUP
;        interrupts disabled
;
; Out:   [ld_lstk] -= entry ax
;        interrupts enabled
;========================================================================
```

(continued on next page)

LISTING 4.3   *(Continued)*

```
        assume  ds:DGROUP,es:nothing,ss:nothing
lname la_adjlstk
        sub     DGROUP:[ld_lstk],ax
        sti
        ret


;================================================================
; la_orig_context
;
; Switch from a local stack back to the caller's stack.
;
; NOTE: A call to la_setlstk must be made one time before
; la_local_context and la_orig_context can be used.
;
; In:    es:bx -> register save area
;        ax = amount to be added to ld_lstk
;
; Out:   caller's registers restored
;        ss:sp -> caller's stack
;================================================================
        assume  ds:nothing,es:nothing,ss:nothing
lname la_orig_context
        pop     es:[bx].onret   ; xfer near return address
        cli
        mov     ss,es:[bx].oss
        mov     sp,es:[bx].osp
        add     sp,2            ; skip orig ss
        mov     bx,seg DGROUP
        mov     ds,bx
        assume  ds:DGROUP
        add     DGROUP:[ld_lstk],ax
        pop     bp
        pop     es
        pop     ds
        pop     di
        pop     si
        pop     dx
        pop     cx
        pop     bx
        pop     ax
        ret
```

LISTING 4.3 *(Continued)*

To use these functions, you must first determine how much stack memory must be allocated to handle each entrance level and how many levels of reentrance are possible. This first factor is referred to as the *stack block allocation*. Together, these two factors determine the total size of the local stack.

For instance, assume that the interrupt intercept–processing code will require a stack of 256 bytes to cover all code executed by the interrupt intercept as well as a reasonable margin for any other interrupts that might occur while this stack is in effect. Assume also that eight reentrance levels are to be supported. From this, you can determine that 2048 bytes would be required for the local stack buffer (256 × 8).

Each time an entrance is made to an intercept where this stack switching code is used, the current value of the [ld_lstk] memory variable is used to set the top of the local stack. Then the stack block allocation is subtracted from this memory variable before interrupts are enabled. This way, if a reentrance should occur, a lower section of the local stack buffer will be used, leaving the stack block in use by the previous entrance layer unchanged.

Listing 4.4 shows how these functions would be used within an interrupt intercept. Note that in this case, a switch back to the local stack is made just before the interrupt call is passed on to the previous vector holder. Upon return from this pass-on call, another switch is made back to the local stack. Then, when the final section of the intercept logic is finished, a switch is made back to the local stack just before the iret is done.

This approach does three things for you. First, the switch back to the local stack, just before the pass-on call, restores the original calling registers, so the previous interrupt handler will see the conditions it expects. Second, in the event that an interrupt handler expects entry data to be on the caller's stack, everything will be in the proper position, just as if the intercept wasn't hooked into the calling chain (the intercept logic previously described would not work in this type of situation). Third, the transplantation of all return registers from the pass-on call is taken care of automatically by the second pair of stack switch calls.

Accessing the Caller's Registers

While the local stack is in effect in the first part of the intercept handler, accessing the original values of the entry registers is simple. Upon exit from the la_local_context function, the ES:BX register pair is pointing to a section of the caller's stack on which all of the caller's registers have been placed. This includes the CS:IP and CPU flags register values that were automatically pushed onto the stack as a result of the software interrupt call.

```
i21_stkblk      equ      256       ; stack block allocation

i21_icept:
        lcall    la_local_context
        mov      ax,i21_stkblk
        lcall    la_adjlstk

; 1st section of intercept logic)

        .....

        mov      ax,i21_stkblk
        lcall    la_orig_context
        pushf
        cli
        call     cs:[i21_orig]
        push     bp
        mov      bp,sp
        pushf                            ; transfer exit flags
        pop      [bp+6]                  ; to stack for iret
        pop      bp
        lcall    la_local_context
        mov      ax,i21_stkblk
        lcall    la_adjlstk

; 2nd section of intercept logic)

        .....

        mov      ax,i21_stkblk
        lcall    la_orig_context
        iret
```

LISTING 4.4   An interrupt intercept with two stack switches

The regset structure for assembler, shown at the top of Listing 4.3, is included within the file \ZLIB\ZLIB.INC on the Companion Diskette. Using this structure in conjunction with the ES:BX register pair, addressing the caller's entry registers is as simple as the following:

```
cmp      es:[bx].osi,1234h
```

It is also possible to write new values to these fields; the new values will be applied to the corresponding registers when the switch is made back to the caller's stack with the `la_orig_context` function. Access to the byte-sized registers (AL, AH, BL, and so on) can be done as well. A common use of this type of access would to test the AH function selector for an interrupt call. For example:

```
cmp     byte ptr es:[bx].oax+1,40h
```

Providing that the ES:BX register pair would always be maintained as the pointer to the caller's register set, a set of equate statements, such as the following could be crafted to simplify register access:

```
_AX     equ     es:[bx].oax
_AH     equ     byte ptr es:[bx].oax+1
_AL     equ     byte ptr es:[bx].oax
_BX     equ     es:[bx].obx
_BH     equ     byte ptr es:[bx].obx+1
```

and so on. It would then be possible to reference the caller's registers with a more simple form of instruction, such as

```
mov     cx,_CX
cmp     _AH,32h
mov     _DL,cs:[new_dl]
```

A complete set of these equate statements is included within the `\ZLIB\ZLIB.INC` file.

Placing the Stack Switch Calls

When these stack-switching functions are used within an interrupt intercept, the call to `la_local_context` must be the first thing in terms of stack depth. No `push` instructions can be placed before this call, unless they are counterbalanced by corresponding `pop` instructions before `la_local_context` is called. Similarly, the call to `la_orig_context` has to be the last operation performed before the final `iret` in terms of stack depth.

In the following code fragment, the use of the ES register was required before the call to `la_local_context`. Since the original stack depth is restored before this function is called, there is no problem with this type of filtering code.

```
        push    es
        mov     es,cs:[xyz_segment]
        cmp     ax,es:[xyz_data]
        pop     es
        je      skip_intercept
        lcall   la_local_context
        .....
        (intercept handler goes here)
        .....
        lcall   la_orig_context
skip_intercept:
        iret
```

By the same token, the following code would work, since no registers are changed and no stack depth changes occur:

```
        cmp     ah,43h
        jne     skip_intercept
        lcall   la_local_context
        ....
        (intercept handler goes here)
        .....
        lcall   la_orig_context
skip_intercept:
        iret
```

The following method would not function correctly. The existence of the BX register on the stack before the call to la_local_context has distorted the stack positioning that this structure was designed to expect.

```
        push    bx
        mov     bx,cs:[xyz]
        cmp     ax,bx
        je      skip_intercept
        lcall   la_local_context
        .....
        (intercept handler goes here)
        .....
        lcall   la_orig_context
skip_intercept:
        pop     bx
        iret
```

The Stack Pocket Technique

In the design of interrupt intercepts, the need can arise for the second section of intercept logic to have access to information derived during the first section. Let's say that you want to construct an INT21 intercept in which entry and exit conditions are reported for each call, including the parameters specific to each call.

A call such as function 47h (get current directory) can pose a small problem. This call accepts a drive number in the DL register and a pointer to a text buffer within DS:SI. Upon completion, this operating system service will have written a string in the text buffer that identifies the current directory for the specified drive.

It will be up to the logic in the second section of the intercept logic (after the pass-on call has been made) to dump this string, but how will the second-section logic determine when the function being called is 47h? Upon completion of this call, DOS changes the AX register (0100h seems to be a typical value). The logic within the second section needs access to the caller's AX value that was extant during execution of the first section.

Listing 4.5 illustrates how a pocket can be formed on the local stack during the first section of an intercept so that data can be passed to the exit section. In this example, the only logic shown within the first section is that which saves the caller's entry AX and CX values, and the only logic shown for the second section is that which accesses these entry values. In an actual intercept handler there would, of course, be additional logic that puts this information to use.

In the example in Listing 4.5, a pocket of 4 bytes is required to make the entry AX and CX values accessible to the second section of intercept logic. This is defined by the i21_pocket equate statement. If your situation involves a large amount of pocket space, be sure to account for this when determining your stack block allocation value.

TSR SPECIFICS

If, when building a TSR, you find a need to allocate additional memory for data storage, there are two basic alternatives. The first is to call DOS's INT21 function 48h memory block allocation function. The consequence of this is that access to this new memory block must be done through far pointers. This data area is not a contiguous extension of the DGROUP data area.

The second alternative is to modify the termination logic to derive a resident paragraph count that takes your additional needs into account. You may wish to study the way this is handled in the init function for the device driver case (see the file \ZLIB\WORK\STOCK\DDSTRTUP.ASM).

```
i21_stkblk      equ     256  ; stack block allocation
i21_pocket      equ     4    ; bytes in section-to-section pocket


i21_orig        dd      ?


i21_icept:
        lcall   la_local_context
        mov     ax,i21_stkblk
        lcall   la_adjlstk
        sub     sp,i21_pocket
        mov     bp,sp           ; setup addressability to pocket

; 1st section of intercept logic

        mov     ax,es:[bx].oax          ; save entry ax
        mov     [bp],ax
        mov     ax,es:[bx].ocx          ; save entry cx
        mov     [bp+2],ax

; adjust the stack while preserving the pocket

        mov     ax,i21_stkblk - i21_pocket
        lcall   la_orig_context
        pushf
        cli
        call    cs:[i21_orig]
        push    bp
        mov     bp,sp
        pushf
        pop     [bp+6]
        pop     bp
        lcall   la_local_context
        mov     ax,i21_stkblk
        lcall   la_adjlstk
        mov     bp,sp           ; setup addressability to pocket
```

(continued on next page)

LISTING 4.5 Preserving stack indormation between sections

```
; 2nd section of intercept logic

        mov     ax,[bp]                 ; recover entry ax
        mov     cx,[bp+2]               ; recover entry cx

; adjust the stack, freeing up the pocket

        mov     ax,i21_stkblk + i21_pocket
        lcall   la_orig_context
        iret
```

LISTING 4.5 *(Continued)*

As with a device driver, there are certain dangers in overlaying the non-resident initialization section of a TSR with what will be additional resident data area. If any action causes this data area to be written to before the initialization process has run to completion, a crash is likely, since the `init` logic will be overwritten. Workable solutions include relocating the final portion of the `init` logic after the overlay buffer or placing the last section of the `init` logic within the resident section.

It is a relatively simple matter to include one or more HLL modules in the construction of a TSR. Using the device driver template and makefile as a guide, the basic idea is to include a `call` and an `extern` statement within the section or sections of the program where an HLL linkage is desired. Proper stack setup for parameters must, of course, be observed. The one critical requirement, for the sake of the link order control scheme, is that once the resident HLL module is compiled, its object module must be processed by the `MODOBJ.EXE` utility before it is linked.

For a ready-made way to establish a C-based interrupt handler or interrupt intercept, see the `c_icept` macro, located in the `\ZLIB\ZLIB.INC` include file.

DEVICE DRIVER SPECIFICS

Device drivers are built using the `.EXE` format, because it can support link order control and mixed-language programming. The `.SYS` extension is used, because using the `.EXE` extension for a device driver can be confusing. The MS-DOS kernel actually doesn't care about the extension—it identifies a driver as an `.EXE` type by a signature within the binary module.

The startup assembler file, `DDSTRTUP.ASM`, should not need to be edited for typical cases. All code and data specific to each driver should be placed within the three files generated by using GETSTOCK.BAT with its SYS parameter. The one common copy of DDSTRTUP.ASM is reassembled each time by the common makefile DDSTOCK.MAK. The processing of this common makefile is brought about by the common batch file MDD.BAT.

Here are the steps required to build a device driver using the templates:

1. Use GETSTOCK SYS *base* to create the three unique files: *base* .DDH, *base* R.C, and *base* T.C.
2. Edit the *base* .DDH file and assign the appropriate values to the fields of the device driver header. The default case is set up for a simple character-type device driver. Refer to books on device driver design for details on character drivers and block drivers.
3. If your driver will make heavy use of stack-based variables, adjust the stack-sizing equates within the *base* .DDH file.
4. Add your driver's nonresident initialization code and data to the *base* T.C module.
5. Add your driver's resident code and data to the *base* R.C module.
6. Build your driver by invoking the MDD.BAT batch file with the driver's basename: MDD *base*.

The only assembler code you have to deal with is in editing the *base* .DDH file. The details of linkage control, stack switching, and load address calculations are all taken care of by the DDSTRTUP.ASM file.

The MDD.BAT batch file invokes your MAKE utility to process the makefile \ZLIB\WORK\STOCK\DDSTOCK.MAK. This common makefile can be used for each device driver you build, provided you do not need to create any additional source files or use a different language. When changes are necessary, you could simply make a unique copy of DDSTOCK.MAK and modify it accordingly. In any case, you will need to modify this stock makefile to match your specific C compiler. The one provided was designed for use with Borland's C/C++ compiler. A copy of DDSTOCK.MAK is shown in Listing 4.6.

Because of the way this makefile is designed to append an r or t to the base filename, the base name is limited to a maximum of seven characters.

One interesting thing to note is that the common startup ASM module, \ZLIB\WORK\STOCK\DDSTRTUP.ASM, is always reassembled any time a driver is linked. This one ASM module will be reused each time you build a different device driver using this book's templates. However, the object module produced in each case is unique, due to the fact that DDSTRTUP.ASM includes the file DDHEADER.INC, which is a copy of your unique file *base* .DDH. The makefile must always reassemble DDSTRTUP.ASM to prevent confusion, since the last copy of DDSTRTUP.OBJ in your working directory could be left over from the creation of a different device driver.

```
#==== macros

# base  = the base name of the source file (7 chars max)
#
# this string must be assigned on the make command line
# using the parameter -Dbase=

tsrc = $(base)t
rsrc = $(base)r

# id for "include directory"

id = c:\zlib

#==== build

$(base).sys    :    $(base).ddh $(rsrc).obj $(tsrc).obj
   copy $(base).ddh ddheader.inc
   masm /Mx /z c:\zlib\work\stock\ddstrtup;
   del ddheader.inc
   tlink ddstrtup $(rsrc) $(tsrc),$(base),$(base)/m,c:\zlib\ztools
   del ddstrtup.obj
   del $(base).sys
   ren $(base).exe $(base).sys

#==== c file obj rules

$(rsrc).obj  :  $(rsrc).c
   bcc -c $&.c
   modobj $&

$(tsrc).obj  :  $(tsrc).c
   bcc -c $&.c
```

LISTING 4.6   The common makefile DDSTOCK.MAK

The dd_init( ) function within the *base* T.C nonresident module has certain responsibilities:

1. The completion status word in the request header must be set.
2. The offset portion of the pointer that describes the driver's end-of-resident point must be prepared.
3. Any load messages must be displayed.

Regarding the completion status, a value of 0100h (0x0100) indicates a normal return with no errors. Use 8000h (0x8000) plus a standard error code value to indicate a failure. See the *MS-DOS Programmer's Reference Manual* or a similar book for details on error codes.

Concerning the reporting of the end-of-resident point, while the final derivation of this value is up to the DDSTRTUP.ASM module, the logic within the *base* T.C module's dd_init( ) function must play a part. If a driver does not require that any extra memory be allocated for buffers, the dd_init( ) function must write a zero into the offset of the ending address pointer. This is taken care of in the stock copy of the *base* T.C module (\ZLIB\WORK\STOCK\DDTSTOCK.C) by the following line:

```
rqpkt->rqinEndAddress.h[0] = 0;
```

See the file \ZLIB\DDSTRUCS.H for a definition of the structures used by the device driver templates to access the driver request header.

If your driver needs to enlarge the resident size of the DGROUP data segment, it should enter the number of bytes needed in this field. When a driver uses this method to declare that it needs more data space, this data area constitutes an overlay onto the code and data of the *base* T.C initialization module. The variable DDTAILPNT holds the offset of the first free byte of this enlarged data area.

If the init code must prepare data in this overlay area, you will have to relocate the init code to a memory position after this area or use a portion of the resident area to hold the last part of the init code. Otherwise, the init code will be overwritten before it has finished its processing.

The only case where a message is displayed is when a completion status word is passed back that indicates an error. The startup code will cause the driver not to be loaded and will issue a short message to that effect. Your code that marks the error should report in more detail.

For the nonerror case, you may want to display a banner identifying the driver, its version number, and any other pertinent status information. The following library functions may be used to display text from within a device driver:

```
void lc_disp_char ( char *dchar )
void lc_disp_str ( char *dchar )
void lc_disp_err_lead ( char *dchar )
```

For more information on these functions, see the files \ZLIB\XLIBDISP .INC, \XLIB\LIBSRC\PUTDISP.C, and \ZLIB\LIBSRC\ZLIB.NDX.

The *base* T.C module comes with an example of implementation of the parsing logic. This one set of library parsing functions can be used in a stand-alone program, TSR, or device driver. If your driver will not need to parse a parameter line, delete this parsing code and the associated data declarations. These sections are marked with comment lines within the template for easy identification. See Chapter 7 for more information on the parsing functions.

If you need or want to build a device driver entirely of assembler code, you could take one of two approaches. First, you could make a copy of the DDSTRTUP.ASM module, remove the external calls to _dd_intr and _dd_init, and add your application-specific code directly to your unique copy of that ASM module. If you also merge a copy of the DDSTOCK.INC header file directly into your assembler file, you could build a device driver by simply assembling and linking that one source file. Because your source code file would be derived from the DDSTRTUP.ASM template, the segment- and group-naming controls would already be established, so the link order control scheme could be used.

To produce a driver from this type of source file, you could write a simple batch file such as this one:

```
masm /mx /z %1;
if errorlevel 1 goto stop
link %1,%1,%1/m, c:\zlib\ztools
if errorlevel 1 goto stop
if exist %1.sys del %1.sys
ren %1.exe %1.sys
:stop
```

The second approach to producing an all-assembler device driver would be to create two files, *base* R.ASM and *base* T.ASM, similar to the .C case. Within the resident file, *base* R.ASM, you would simply create a public function named _ddintr and fashion it to receive the parameters as set up by the startup module. Within the *base* T.ASM file for the nonresident section, you would then create a function named _ddinit. In case, you should make a unique copy of the DDSTOCK.MAK file and replace the C compilation commands with assembler commands.

THE MODOBJ.EXE UTILITY

Another significant feature of the DDSTOCK.MAK makefile is the use of the MODOBJ.EXE utility in creating the .OBJ module for the resident section. This utility program reads in an object module containing standard segment names, _TEXT, _DATA, and _BSS, and produces a new copy of the object module in which the segment names have been modified to RTEXT, RDATA, and RBSS. Certain other segment control strings are modified as well.

The source to the MODOBJ.EXE utility is included on the Companion Diskette. This utility is also used to build libraries that conform to the link order control scheme.

USING OTHER HIGH-LEVEL LANGUAGES

While the device driver templates are designed to use C code for the actual working portions, the working portion could be produced from any other language that can generate a "pure" object module with "conforming" segment and group names. A "pure" object module is one that contains no built-in startup code or standard library code—only the code and data for your specific source language statements. A "conforming" object module is one that uses segment and group names matching those used by a typical small-model C module: _TEXT for the code segment and _DATA and _BSS for the data segments, where the data segments are both within the group DGROUP.

If your compiler of choice uses different segment names, you will have to edit the templates and library files to match, modify the MODOBJ utility, and then rebuild the library.

STACK ISSUES REVISITED

In both the device driver and TSR templates, the stack-switching functions are declared as external from within the resident section. If your project won't need them, delete the lextrn statements to reduce the size of the binary module by a couple of hundred bytes. If your project will need to switch to a local stack only during the initialization function, you could simply use the explicit stack switch code already in place: Just delete any calls to la_setlstk and move the stack allocation from the RDATA segment to the _DATA segment. When no local stack is needed at all, delete the stack allocation statements altogether.

Within the `init` function of DDSTRTUP.ASM, you will notice that it does a simple type of stack switch rather than use the `la_local_context` function. This is done for two reasons. First, this simpler form is acceptable in this situation, because reentrance is not an issue. Second, with the `la_local_context` and `la_orig_context` functions linked into the resident section, a call from the nonresident section would require a version of these functions designed for far calling.

It is not possible to use the `la_gpcsh` far-calling shell function with the stack-switching functions. To do so would be inviting a crash, since the new stack that was switched to would not contain the necessary return address.

Within the stack setup of DDSTRTUP.ASM's `init` logic, notice also that two calls are made to the `la_setlstk` function instead of just one. The first call defines the starting point of the local stack that will be used in the event that a call is made to `la_local_context` during the time the initialization logic is running. This could happen if the resident section contained any hardware interrupt handlers that could be entered while the `_dd_init` function is also using the local stack.

To prevent a stack collision in this event, the first call to `la_setlstk` is made with a value that is below the top of the local stack by the amount of the equated term NONRES_BLK_SIZE (defined within the *base*.DDH include file). The value of this term controls the portion of the stack that is reserved for use by the initialization logic. If your init logic will make heavy use of the stack, and if it is possible for `la_local_context` to be called during the initialization process, you should increase the size of memory associated with this term.

As shown in the following code excerpts, when the `init` logic has run to completion and the local stack is no longer being used, a second call is made to the `la_setlstk` function. This is done to allow the entire local stack to be used by any subsequent calls to `la_local_context`.

- Starting section of the `_dd_init` function:

```
cli
mov     [origss],ss
mov     [origsp],sp
mov     ss,ax
mov     sp,offset dgroup:stack_top
sti
mov     ax,offset dgroup:stack_top-nonres_blk_size
lcall   la_setlstk
```

- Ending section of the _dd_init function:

```
cli
mov     ss,[origss]
mov     sp,[origsp]
sti
mov     ax,offset dgroup:stack_top
lcall   la_setlstk
```

If you modify the init logic of a TSR to include switching to a local stack, and if reentrance is possible, you should consider using this protected method.

CHAPTER 5
Building Libraries

IDENTIFYING LIBRARY CANDIDATES

Whenever a function is needed in more than one program, serious consideration should be given to relocating that function to a library. General-purpose functions that present menus and manage display windows are prime examples.

Libraries can also be appropriate in an application-specific sense. You may have functions that you'd never use outside of a particular object but do use in several different programs involved in that project. Such functions can be placed into a project-specific library just as general functions are placed into one or more general-purpose libraries.

The majority of candidate functions are created during the development of actual software tools and applications. When designing and coding a tool, watch for any functions that are general-purpose or could be segmented into a general-purpose portion and a tool-specific portion. The basic question to ask yourself when considering a function for library membership: "In what other situation could this function be used?"

When you first identify a function as a library candidate, it's a good time to forget anything you know about it at a detailed level and step back to develop a general concept. Viewing the function at a higher level can help you see things that you may miss if you stay in the high-detail realm. Consider how the function could be used in other programs besides the tool you're currently developing. This can help you see where parameters should be added or modified. You might realize that the function should be split into a family of smaller functions.

When it does appear that a division is in order, list each of the processes involved and then allot them to their respective groups. Then identify the minimum interface that these newly divided sections require to interoperate and still satisfy the overall process. Reconsider these interfaces, since each of these new functions should be generalized. Finally, reapply this black-box analysis method to each of these new pieces.

An Example of Layering

A typical on-line help system involves a text file browser that displays a window and automatically presents the appropriate portion of a text file. Let's look at the functionality needed and come up with a breakdown of the functional blocks. We would need the following:

- A file browser function that opens a display window, loads the appropriate portion of the help file, displays the text, and responds to keyboard commands
- A function that searches an index list of file offsets keyed by a mnemonic tag string, returning the associated file offset
- A function that loads the index file into memory
- Low-level functions to open windows, display text, and get keyboard input

Once you've broken the candidate process down into its functional blocks, identify which are specific to this process and which are general. The low-level windowing, display, and keyboard functions would, of course, be common. The index file–loading and–searching functions would probably be specific to this particular library module. These helper functions would be private in scope, meaning that they would not be known to any other library functions or to the main program. A library module may include private global data and private helper functions, so don't think that a function that calls other functions or uses global variables cannot be placed in a library.

The process of loading a text file into a buffer for browsing could be designed as an independent library function. This would mean, however, that the keyboard-prompting logic would be located within the browsing function. What if, in addition to the file-browsing control keys (PgUp, PgDn, Home, End, up arrow, and down arrow), you must also respond to other keys?

In an on-line help system, you might want a function key to open a second window containing an index of help topics. Selecting a topic from this list would change the text being viewed in the first help window. Support for hypertext features could also be a requirement, where certain words are highlighted and can be selected to change the text being viewed.

To handle such features, you might think you'd need to create a file-browsing logic specifically designed to support these features. There is another approach, Which allows a simple file browser function to form the basis for operations that require specific keyboard responses. Hook calls can be designed into a general-purpose browser function to support extensibility. This makes it possible to respond to additional keystroke actions, to affect the section of the file being displayed, and to affect the attributes of the display and the location of the cursor. Hook calls are studied in more detail further in this chapter.

Shell Processes

You might encounter cases where a process is a good candidate for library inclusion, except that some internal portion of it is application-specific. A directory search loop is a common example. The details of calling find-first and find-next directory search functions are common, but the action taken with each file found is application-specific. This is another situation well suited to the use of a hook function.

You could make a general-purpose library function to handle directory search processing. The address of a work function would also be passed to this function in addition to search specification parameters. For each file found, the work function would be called and be passed information such as the file's name, size, and other directory attributes.

Another example of a shell type of process is parameter parsing. The overall process of parameter parsing is general, and therefore a good candidate for a library inclusion, but the validation of each type of parameter is situation-specific. Chapter 7 presents a set of parsing functions that use function hooks. These functions are also provided on the Companion Diskette.

DESIGNING FUNCTIONS FOR LIBRARY INCLUSION

First, a word about function name prefixes. You may notice that all functions in the Companion Library start with either `la_` or `lc_` (for example, `lc_getkey()`). The use of the `la_` prefix does not mean that the function was written in assembler. Rather, it means that the function is designed to be called from assembler—that is, it has an assembler-style interface. (In most cases, such functions *would* also be written in assembler.) Likewise, the `lc_` prefix means that the function is designed to be called from C. These functions could be written in C or assembler.

These prefixes are required for libraries compatible with the link order control scheme. If you will not be building any TSRs or device drivers, you won't need link order control, but the use of function prefixes can still be helpful because it distinguishes library functions and helps prevent naming conflicts. See the section on Link Order Control for more information on the use of the la_ and lc_ prefixes.

Bottom-Up Design

Many library functions must use lower-level functions for display output, keyboard input, and other common operations. These foundation functions must, of course, be established before other functions are written that use them. For this reason, libraries are built from the bottom up rather than from the top down. Your options are to write your own low-level functions, to use standard library functions included with your language package, or to use a third-party library.

The most important thing is consistency. Having some video display functions, from a standard library, that use a default attribute; others, in a third-party library, that use a globally set attribute; and still others, in your own library, that use attributes supplied with each call would be confusing.

Regarding keyboard input, if calls to the BIOS's INT16 services are used in some library functions (rather than INT21-based keyboard input services), input redirection could not be used with any tools built from such a library.

Planning for Future Growth

There are three basic ways to support expansion:

1. Design calling hooks into a function.
2. Establish a well-thought-out calling hierarchy.
3. Anticipate future parameter needs and design them into your function's initial interface, even though the actual implementation for these parameters may not be filled out yet.

The first two items will be investigated more fully in upcoming sections. It is the third item that we'll focus on here. As an example, let's consider a function that reports on the status of a certain resource. When first implemented, the output required of this function may fit into a single byte or word, and therefore could be passed back to the point of call as the function's return value:

```
current_status = get_status ( dataset1 )
```

But if you know that additional status information will be required in the future, you would be wise to accommodate that situation from the start. This could be done by designing the function to accept a pointer to a status information structure. The function would write the appropriate status information using this structure pointer before returning:

```
stat_ptr = &stat_record
get_status ( dataset1, stat_ptr )
```

With this approach, a structure can be defined at first to contain only a byte or word and be expanded later. At that future time, all modules that reference the structure and call the status-reporting function would need to be recompiled, but only the calling points that need to process additional status information would need to be recoded. Since the interface itself will not need to change, there would be no need to change all calling points, as would be the case if the first method was used.

If a data structure such as this must be defined in some permanent form, you should allocate a dummy array within it to reserve room for future expansion. For example, consider the case of a TSR that contains a status-reporting function and uses a software interrupt handler as a means of communications with other programs. If you were to supply this module to a user base and specify that only one byte of status information is returned, your users would then develop programs that make use of this TSR utility and design their calls for a one-byte return value.

If, at some future point, you need additional status information to be returned by that same function, you'll have to talk your existing customers into recoding their programs. It would be better to have told them from the start that your status function requires the address of a status data structure of a certain predetermined size. If it is too difficult to come up with a reserved size factor ahead of time, you could specify an interface where status information structures must be allocated from a heap using a size value obtained from another status call.

It may seem as though it would take longer to imagine these other cases now and put in features that you don't currently need, but, if it is at all likely that you will someday need them, it probably won't be a waste of time. If you have to change a library function's interface after it is already in use, you'll have to go back and modify all tools that make use of this function. Then you'll have to retest all of these modified programs to verify that no undesirable side effects have been introduced. This can be a significant problem even when all affected programs are under your control. When programs developed by others are involved, you're risking a strained relationship with these other developers.

Error Handling

An important part of designing library functions is error control. During the high-level design phase, consider what errors could occur and plan for them. Keep track of what processing has been done at each error point, so that you can design code that takes compensating action or document the need for this action on the part of the caller.

The following are common error-handling tasks:

- Reset hardware to a known state.
- Free heap memory.
- Close files.
- Reset private global variables within the library module.

The need to free allocated resources, such as heap memory, depends on your situation and error-handling philosophy. If an error is sure to cause termination, you don't have to worry about deallocating any heap memory used by the library function, provided that the allocation does not persist after the program terminates. If a library function could be used in a program where error recovery would be attempted, this library module should either deallocate its memory or leave a record saying that it remains allocated from the previous operation cycle. In some cases, you might want to make a separate library function for deallocation and have application-specific code decide when to call it upon detecting an error return code.

As a resource allocation–tracking method, you could use one or more words of bit flags, setting a particular bit as each resource is committed. The error-handling logic would then test each bit for a 1 state and take appropriate action.

Where pointers to heap blocks are involved, an alternate method is to ensure that all pointers hold a NULL value when not pointing to an allocated block of heap memory. Then, when an error occurs, a free() call can be made for each non-NULL pointer.

Regarding function return codes, if you want or need different return codes to be passed back for each situation, it gets complicated when one function calls another that passes back a variety of codes itself. Allocating non overlapping codes to each function becomes a maintenance nightmare as new functions are added and existing ones modified.

One approach is to maintain global variables that identify the function where the error originated and hold a specific error code describing the situation. With this method, each function would simply return with a nonzero return code. When an error is detected within a deeply nested calling hierarchy, each library function would simply return to its caller with this simple type of error signal. When the calling chain finally unwinds to the point where errors are decoded and processed, the global variables would hold the right information.

The storage and display of error message strings is another relevant issue. When a library function is already in use to display other messages for the nonerror case, it can be used to display error messages as well. When this isn't the case, it is unwise to invoke display functions such as `printf()` or `puts()` only for error messages. It might be the only reference to those functions in the program, adding extra code when the main part of the program is using a different display method. It also might be necessary to use a specific display method in different applications.

To provide a flexible error-reporting mechanism, consider developing a library function for that purpose. Display output can be handled through a function hook, making it simple to adapt the display output method for different situations. Centralization of message display activities will also be important if you are developing a product that must support multiple languages.

Information Hiding, Encapsulation, and Abstraction

Let's start with some definitions:

Information hiding—Ensuring that nonessential aspects of a process or data are inaccessible.

Abstraction—Representing a process or data so that only the essential aspects are made public; communicating only what is necessary to initiate a process without requiring that the caller know anything about the algorithm, its implementation, or any internal data.

Encapsulation—The actualization of information hiding. Bonding together of code and data and considering them as one object.

Employing these design ideas in your software helps to prevent unwanted side effects, produces more robust and independent functions, and reduces the amount of detail with which you must contend when using established library functions.

Some additional benefits are:

- Improved readability
- Easier maintenance
- Easier debugging
- Refinement of internal code without affecting the calling interface
- Easier code reuse
- Easier control of complexity

Private and Public

What are the mechanics of information hiding? Languages designed to support an object-oriented approach have their own methods of declaring and defining functions and data. Ultimately, it comes down to which function names and variable names are made public and which are not.

In assembler, variables and functions are private by default (nonpublic). You must use the PUBLIC keyword to make them accessible to other modules. For example:

```
widget_size  dw  0  ; this one will be private

public widget_type

widget_type  dw  0  ; this one will be public
```

In standard C, the opposite is true. Functions are public by default, and you must use the static keyword to make them private. This same rule applies to global variables. Although the static keyword can be applied to local variables (also called automatic variables), these variables are never made public. When the static keyword is used with a local variable, it becomes nonautomatic, meaning that it will retain its value even when the function it is defined in exits.

When a library module has only one function, if a variable is needed that will hold its data between calls, you can use a static local variable or a private global variable. A global variable is indicated for the case where a library module will contain multiple functions, where each needs access to common data. The reason for using the static keyword with a global variable is to prevent any other modules from being able to refer to it—to keep it properly hidden. This can also help prevent naming conflicts.

At this point, it becomes important to distinguish between a data definition and a data declaration. A data definition generates an instance where storage is actually allocated. A declaration is a reference to the defining instance—a description of the type of data involved.

Private Global Variables

A private global variable is a variable that is global in scope to each of the functions within a library module but is private to that module. Direct access to this variable by code outside of the library module is not possible.

Once you hide data, you must take different steps to initialize it. A common approach is to have an initializer function within the library module itself. Such a function can contain a simple assignment logic, copying passed-in parameter values directly into the library module-specific global variables, or it could perform more derivation and validation processing on the data first.

If you would provide a function to return the current value of a private global variable, consider how that information will be used. In the case of a family of direct video display functions, you may want to support access to the segment of the video buffer in order to tell application code whether a monochrome or a color display is being used.

Rather than reporting the B000 or B800 segment value directly, you may wish to make a function that returns a flag to indicate monochrome or color. This way, if you need to accommodate monochrome VGA or adapt to some new type of video adapter in the future, you will have to change only the implementation, not the interface or the calling code.

A similar consideration would apply for the initialization function for this type of private global variable. While you could write application code to determine the segment of the video buffer and call a simple assignment function, it would be better to centralize the video buffer detection logic within a library module. When future types of video adapters are introduced, where a different determination method is used, only the function's implementation will require modification.

Using an initializer in a variable's definition is convenient and appropriate for many cases. Within a library module written in C, a definition including an initializer could look like this:

```
static word last_line = 0xffff;
```

In this case, a word variable named `last_line` is being initialized to the value 0xFFFF. In certain situations, however, this method will cause problems. Consider the case of a file-browsing function that maintains a global variable to hold the line number of the last line in the file. Until the file has been browsed through to its end, this value cannot be known, so `last_line` simply holds its initial value of 0xFFFF.

As you page down through a file's text, more lines are read and buffered until an EOF condition is detected. At this point, `last_line` is set and can then be used to regulate the display actions of the browser. If this private global variable is defined and initialized as just shown, the browser would exhibit a strange bug, as the following example shows:

1. The file-browsing function is called to operate on a 100-line file. Since the user does scroll the text through to the end, `last_line` becomes assigned the value 100.
2. The browsing operation is terminated, and control returns to the main program.

3. Later on in that same program, the file-browsing function is called again, but this time the file contains 150 lines.

Since the `last_line` variable still holds the value of 100 from the previous invocation, rather than the initial value of 0xFFFF that the EOF detection logic is designed to work with, this 150-line file will appear to have only 100 lines. In a case like this, `last_line` should be declared without an initializer, and the entry logic of the browser function should be made to assign the initial value of 0xFFFF to it.

Public Global Variables

Although this is counter to a strict information hiding policy, you may sometimes want a global variable within a library module to be public.

Let's consider again the case of a family of video display functions that use the direct video–writing method. A main library module contains global variables to define the video segment, the offset of the current write point (`lc_vptr`), and the number of display lines (`lc_vrows`) and columns (`lc_vcols`). This first module also contains a function named `lc_init_vid_data` to derive the initial values for these public variables.

A second module contains the function `lc_char2vid`, which writes a character to the display buffer, using the current value of `lc_vptr`, and then advances `lc_vptr`, to the next position (the issue of video scrolling is ignored here for simplicity). A third module contains a pair of video functions that save and restore selected regions of the screen. These functions are used to support pop-up window–type interfaces and are packaged together because it makes little sense for one to be used without the other.

Each of the functions in these latter two modules does require access to the global data within the first module. To operate efficiently, these modules should be able to access the direct video pointer directly. An `extrn` (assembler) or `extern` (C) statement would be used within each to declare that the reference to the `lc_vptr` variable requires that another object module be found that has a public record for that variable.

Here are the three modules:

```
lib module 1: global video data and primitive functions

dword lc_vptr
word lc_vrows
word lc_vcols

        lc_init_vid_data
```

```
┌─ lib module 2: write a character

│   ┌─ lc_char2vid
│   └
└

┌─ lib module 3: save and restore screen data

│   ┌─ lc_save_region
│   └
│   ┌─ lc_restore_region
│   └
└
```

Using public global library variables, where the only type of access intended is by a family of library modules, is perfectly acceptable. Just stick to the rules and don't access these public global variables directly from your application programs.

Granularity

The rule of thumb on function granularity is simple: If it is at all practical to make a separate library module for each function, do so. While this does result in a greater number of library source and object modules, each program you build can be smaller since only the functions actually needed will be linked in. As seen in the foregoing section on public global variables, the fact that all the members of a family of functions need access to common global data does not mean that they must all be located within the same module.

In the third module in the preceding example, the lc_save_region and lc_restore_region functions were grouped together in one library module because they will always be used together. Other reasons to group functions together in the same module would be if they shared any private helper functions or private global data.

Private Helper Functions

When designing a library module, you will sometimes want to make certain functions private. These would be functions used only as helpers to the public function or functions of the library module. For example, the public function of a module might be lc_rec_size(), a function that determines the size of a certain variable-length type of record. Internally, this function may make calls to a helper function named `align_rec()`. This helper function is not useful as a stand-alone library function—it is used only within `lc_rec_size()`.

Since functions are private by default in assembler, you simply don't code a `public` statement for a helper function:

```
lib module: recsiz.asm

public lc_rec_size

    lc_rec_size


    align_rec
```

In C, the opposite is true. All functions are public by default. The `static` keyword must be used to make a function private:

```
libmodule: recsiz.c

    word lc_rec_size ()


    static void align_rec ()
```

FUNCTION HOOKS

A function hook provides a way for you to control the internal operation of a library module. Function hooks work through a mechanism known as a *function pointer* or *call vector*. In C, the following statement defines a function pointer named `hook1`:

```
static void (hook1 *)();
```

Once the address of a function is assigned to this pointer, calling it through the pointer is quite similar to making a direct call:

```
void display_msg ( byte *sptr )
{

  puts ( sptr );
}

hook1 = display_msg;

(hook1)( "this is it\n" ); /* same as display_msg("...")*/
```

In assembler, this could be done as:

```
hook1   dw  ?

        mov  [hook1],offset display_msg

        call [hook1]    ; same as call display_msg
```

To understand the benefit of this indirect calling method, let's jump right into some real-world examples.

Video Driver Hooks

Suppose that you need a group of display output functions capable of operating through direct video, BIOS INT10 calls, or output to a serial port to a terminal. For simplicity, let's consider only the member of this group of functions that displays a single character at the current cursor position, ignoring for now the other functions that would be necessary (such as to clear the screen or to change the cursor position).

In specific, what is required is a library function that presents one generic interface but can be made to carry out its internal processing in different ways. A simple (hence limited) approach would be to build a function that uses a control variable to decide which output method to use. This control variable, named display_method, would be a private global variable.

```
┌─ lib module: dispchr
│
│  static byte display_method
│
│  ┌─ void display_method ( byte outm_value )
│  │
│  │  display_method = outm_value
│  └──
```

```
void display_char ( byte dchar )

    switch ( display_method )

        case 1 :
        display dchar using direct video
        break

        case 2 :
        display dchar using BIOS INT10
        break

        case 3 :
        transmit dchar to the serial terminal
        break
```

This approach has the following limitations:

- Processing time is required for each character to determine which method to use.
- It is not easily extensible. Additional output methods cannot be created without modifying the library module.
- The library module will always hold extra code.

Redesigning this module to use a function hook addresses each of these limitations. The code for each type of display output is located in a separate library module, so only those modules actually referenced will be linked into the final program. Further, it would even be possible for a program using the dispchr library module to assign an application-specific driver function to the display_hook function vector.

```
lib module: dispchr

static void (display_hook *) ()

    void set_ display_method ( void (hook_value *) () )

    display_hook = hook_value
```

```
    ┌── void display_char ( byte dchar )
    │
    │  (display_hook) (dchar)
    │└──
    │
    └──


  ┌── lib module: dispvid
  │
  │  ┌── void dispchar_vid ( byte dchar )
  │  │   display dchar using direct video
  │  │└──
  │  │
  │  └──
  └──


  ┌── lib module: dispi10
  │
  │  ┌── void dispchar_i10 ( byte dchar )
  │  │   display dchar using BIOS INT10
  │  │└──
  │  │
  │  └──
  └──


  ┌── lib module: dispser
  │
  │  ┌── void dispchar_ser ( byte dchar )
  │  │   transmit dchar to the serial terminal
  │  │└──
  │  │
  │  └──
  └──
```

Getkeys Hooks

In the preceding example, the `display_hook` function call vector had to be assigned the address of a low-level video driver function or no display output would result. Indeed, the system would crash if the `display_char()` function were called before a meaningful value was assigned to its function hook variable.

Function hooks can also play an important role in another sense, in which establishing a hook is optional rather than required. A prime example is a function used to obtain a character from the keyboard. By implanting a set of hooks in this type of function, it is possible to support a variety of useful features such as:

- Hot-key support (such as for pop-up help windows)
- Mouse emulation of cursor keys
- Keystroke macros
- Background printing

While console input processing is studied in much greater depth in Chapter 7, we will take a brief look at it here to further illustrate the use of function hooks. Of the several hook points involved, the one of interest here is known as the keyboard-idle hook.

When a function is called to wait for the next available keyboard character, an opportunity for background processing, such as printing, exists. The basic idea is to interject a call to a hook function within the keyboard-polling loop. Here's a simple model:

```
lib module: getkeys

static void (idle_hook *) () = hook1_default;

    static void hook1_default ()


    void set_idle_hook ( void (hook_value *) () )

    idle_hook = hook_value;


    byte getkey ( void )

    byte key_value

        while ( 1 )

            if ( a key is ready )

            read the key into key_value
            return ( key_value )

            else
            (idle_hook) ()
```

Within the getkey() function, whenever keystroke data is not available, repeated calls are made to the idle_hook function vector. This variable's definition includes an initializer, which assigns the address of `hook1_default()`. Since the `hook1_default()` function is an empty function, no background processing action will occur—the `getkey()` function will act like a simple hang-for-a-key type of function.

Now let's say that a call is made to the `set_idle_hook()` function to assign the address of a printing function:

```
byte printing_active

    void printing_hook ( void )

        if ( printing_active )

            if ( not eof )
            read a small buffer of data from
             the file to be printd
            output the buffer to the printer

            else
            printing_active = 0
            close the file


    word main ()

    printing_active = 0
    set_idle_hook ( printing_hook )

    ....
    ....
    make calls to getkey ()
    ....
        if ( printing command detected )
        open file
        printing_active = 1

    ....
```

When a certain menu choice was selected or other type of command entered, the main command-decoding logic would initiate a background printing job by opening the file containing the information to be printed and setting the `printing_active` flag. The next time the system is waiting for keystroke information and so makes repeated calls to the `printing_hook()` function, those calls will print the file a buffer at a time. As a result, productive use is made of otherwise wasted time.

Function Hook Wrap-up

In some cases, you may want to read the address currently in a function hook vector so that a calling chain can be established. This is basically the same idea as an intercept of an interrupt vector. Each hook function would have to be designed to call the previous vector holder. This could be applied in the foregoing example if multiple types of background processing were required.

If your chosen language doesn't support pointers to functions, you could design a library function to call a function that is expected to exist within your program. While this isn't as flexible as the function hook method, it will support the same type of processing.

Another alternative is to develop an assembler function that is passed the address of the function to be called. Passing parameters in this situation is, however, less convenient, since you must either arrange for each case's parameter-passing requirements with an individual assembler calling shell or adopt a generic parameter-passing method.

TESTING LIBRARY FUNCTIONS

Before incorporating a function into a library, place it in a test bed and give it a thorough round of shakedown testing. Use all reasonable variety of valid and invalid input and operating conditions. Determine boundary conditions for input parameters, global parameters, and private internal data as well as output data.

In the calling portion of a test bed, you can set up nested loops to generate permutations of values for multiple variables. Include logic that will output a report for each trial to standard output. For each trial, input and output parameters should be shown, along with internal data and execution flow states where appropriate.

When you have a known good trial, save the file along with a copy of the test bed code. Once you finally add the function to your library, make a copy of the test bed program, deleting the local version of the function so that the new library version will be used. Then rerun your tests and verify that the same conditions are reported.

It is wise to keep each test bed and output file in an archive, so that whenever changes must be made to a library function, you can easily determine how the new behavior differs from the last tested state. Use a module comment block at the start of the source file that tells what module the test bed is for and a summary of the testing it does. The STANDA.ASM and STANDC.C templates are often useful in constructing test bed programs.

TRADITIONAL LIBRARIES AND LINK ORDER CONTROL

Within the set of library functions included on this book's Companion Diskette, the following naming convention is used:

- Functions prefixed with la_ are designed to be called from within assembler programs (for example la_setlstk).
- Functions prefixed with lc_ are designed to be called from within C programs (for example lc_passon()).

Strictly speaking, these prefixes are necessary only when you need to take advantage of the link order control scheme. In any case, it can be helpful to use some sort of prefix for library functions. Doing so helps prevent name conflicts with built-in functions (those supplied with a language package), with other library functions, and with application-specific functions you write for each program. The use of a prefix also acts as an indicator that a function comes from a certain library.

If you never intend to produce program modules with resident and nonresident sections, you can ignore the considerations for link order control. You don't need to run the MODOBJ.EXE utility within your makefile; you don't need to limit your library module filenames to seven characters, and you don't need to have the TLIBDEFS.H file included in C programs (delete the include statement for it within \ZLIB\ZLIB.H). In assembler, you don't need the LCALL and LNAME macros, but you still may want to have an underscore prepended to each library function to simplify mixing with C code.

Header Files

Where HLL functions are to be separately compiled and placed into libraries, the use of header files is often necessary. The compiler needs a prototype declaration for each public library function in order to know how to generate the appropriate calling code and to verify that the proper types of parameters are being used at each call point.

Note that, at least in C, it is not necessary to maintain a one-to-one correspondence between libraries and header files. For example, a library may contain 50 object modules, each of which holds a single function. But rather than have one header file containing 50 function prototypes, it is often more wise to section them up.

If 12 of the functions are related to video display management, place their prototype information in one header file. For another twenty functions that support graphics printing, create a new header file, and so on until all functions have been accounted for. Paying attention to granularity in header files is helpful in reducing compile time, just as having granular libraries helps reduce code size.

In this sizing and grouping of header information, there is an issue of balance. Too many small header files will increase compile time, due to the additional file-open operations involved. Conversely, too few large header files waste the time reading and parsing more declarations than will be used in a given program.

Within header files, it is wise not to rely on any defaults when declaring function prototypes. If a C function returns type int, declare it as such rather than relying on the default assumption that type int is used when no explicit declaration is provided. In C, the cdecl keyword specifies the standard C type of stack processing for parameter-passing in function calls (in contrast to the pascal keyword, which specifies a different stack interface technique). While the cdecl function type is the default when no explicit specification is made, it is safest to be explicit in each function's prototype declaration.

If you place your header files in the same directory as your compiler's built-in header files, the compiler will find them easily, but this means more maintenance whenever you upgrade compilers. You must keep track of which headers are to be replaced and which must be preserved.

It's better to put your header files in the directory where the corresponding library file is built. You will be specifying that path within the makefile anyway. Whatever you do, avoid writing include statements that contain explicit drive and path specifications. If you ever need to rearrange your disk's structure, you'll regret it.

Many compilers support a switch to designate search paths for include files. Borland's C compiler uses the −I switch to specify header file search directories.

GENERATING A LIBRARY

The only sane way to deal with library generation is to automate the task with a make utility. The idea is, of course, to produce an object module from a

source code module and use a library utility to add that .OBJ file to the
.LIB file. Microsoft language packages come with a librarian by the name of
LIB.EXE. Borland's library utility is named TLIB.EXE.

Using a makefile means that you can edit any of the source files to fix
bugs and add new features; when you're done, each module that was changed
will be reassembled or recompiled and the resulting object module inserted
into the library file in place of the previous version of that same module.

Below is the basic syntax to be used to add an object module to a library:

```
tlib libname -+objname
```

The minus operator specifies that the named object module should be deleted
from the library. The plus operator then designates that the current copy of
that object module be added to the library. The net result is that the library
has one of its object modules refreshed. When a library is first built, the minus
operator will cause an error message to display saying that the module doesn't
exist. This can be ignored.

Listing 5.1 shows a makefile for a simple library, where the link order
control scheme is not incorporated. In this example, two C files and two
assembler files are involved. Name substitution macros are used to isolate the
points at which explicit directory paths appear. This both simplifies the task
of modifying the location used and reduces clutter within the makefile.

To add a new object module to a library, simply edit its makefile and
enter the .OBJ filename after the all target. Then make a corresponding
entry within the "c dependencies" or "asm dependencies" section.

Listing 5.2 shows a version of this makefile adapted to support the
link order control scheme. Notice that when one of the implicit rules fires
(.c.obj or .asm.obj), the object module is first added to the library in its
original form, then processed by the MODOBJ.EXE utility and added to the
library a second time with an r appended to the end of the object module's
filename.

LIBRARY MAINTENANCE TIPS

If you make a change to a common header file and one or more object
modules of a library and then want to rerun the makefile, all object modules
that depend on the common header file will be rebuilt. To prevent the extra
time this can take, especially in a large library, use a touch utility to make the
directory date and time for each object module be newer than the common
header file. You must then delete the .OBJ files for each module that should
be rebuilt by the make process.

```
#==== name substitution macros

libname = \zlib\ztools.lib

# id for "include directory"

id = \zlib

#==== implicit rules

.c.obj:
   bcc -c $&.c
   tlib $(libname)-+$&.obj

.asm.obj:
   masm /mx /z $&;
   tlib $(libname) -+$&.obj

#==== cause each rule to be examined

all :     inset.obj   touppr.obj   \
          strcpy.obj   strlen.obj

#==== c dependencies

inset.obj   : inset.c      $(id)\zlib.h
touppr.obj  : touppr.c     $(id)\zlib.h

#==== asm dependencies

strcpy.obj  : strcpy.asm  $(id)\zlib.inc
strlen.obj  : strlen.asm  $(id)\zlib.inc
```

LISTING 5.1 A makefile for a simple library

If you rename or delete a library module, you will, of course, need to edit the makefile. You will also need to use the library utility program to manually delete the old copy of the module from the library. If you are building a link order control–based library, be sure to delete both versions of the object module.

```
#==== name substitution macros

libname = \zlib\ztools.lib

# id for "include directory"

id = \zlib

# df for "def file"

df = $(id)\zlibdefs.h

#==== implicit rules

.c.obj:
    bcc -c $&.c
    tlib $(libname) -+&.obj
    del $&r.obj
    ren $&.obj $&r.obj
    modobj $&r
    tlib $(libname) -+$&r.obj
    ren $&r.obj $&.obj

.asm.obj:
    masm /mx /z $&;
    tlib $(libname) -+$&.obj
    del $&r.obj
    ren $&.obj $&r.obj
    modobj $&r
    tlib $(libname) -+$&r.obj
    ren $&r.obj $&.obj
```

(continued on next page)

LISTING 5.2 A makefile for a link order library

```
#==== cause each rule to be examined

all :     inset.obj   touppr.obj  \
          strcpy.obj  strlen.obj

#==== c dependencies

inset.obj   : inset.c     $(id)\zlib.h $(df)
touppr.obj  : touppr.c    $(id)\zlib.h $(df)

#==== asm dependencies

strcpy.obj  : strcpy.asm   $(id)\zlib.inc
strlen.obj  : strlen.asm   $(id)\zlib.inc
```

LISTING 5.2   *(Continued)*

CHAPTER 6
Documentation Management

We all want and appreciate quality documentation in the programs and library modules that we work with. How to write effective documentation is a topic that warrants much more coverage than this one chapter. The issues to be treated here are where to keep your documentation and how to manage access to it.

If you maintain software documentation in a file separate from the corresponding source code, it is possible to develop one master documentation file, which covers all modules for a library, a large, multimodule program, or a group of programs. When you're not sure which module contains the code you need, you can just browse through that one master file.

On the other hand, when you need to review or make changes to a piece of software, having all pertinent documentation contained directly within the source file is best. When you are deeply involved in analysis of existing code, you don't want to have to track down documentation in another file. Further, once you've made changes to a piece of code, you are more likely to make corresponding updates to the documentation the easier it is for you to make them.

You can have best of both worlds by using a documentation extraction system. This approach allows you to maintain the original documentation directly within the source file, where it's easy to find. Then, whenever you want, you can run a text-processing tool that reads your source code files, locates the documentation blocks, and places copies of each in one common text file. This common file can then be loaded into an editor or browser, or you could use it as the source text with an on-line help utility that provides access to your program and library documentation at the touch of a hot key.

EXTRACT.EXE—BASIC OPERATION

A program named EXTRACT.EXE is provided on the Companion Diskette. This utility reads each line of an input text file and copies selected lines to an output text file. Special marker lines control which portions of the input file are copied to the output file.

Through command line parameters, you can specify which text files to scan, the type of marker to watch for, and the output filename. To get a better idea of how this works, let's consider a simple example. Let's say that the ten following lines are contained within a file named SRC.TXT.

```
line 01
line 02
,fs
line 04
line 05
line 06
,fe
line 08
line 09
line 10
```

When EXTRACT.EXE reads each of the lines in this file, it will recognize the third line as a start-of-extraction marker (the line containing the ,fs string). A copy of all successive lines will be appended to the specified output file until the end-of-extraction marker in line 7 is encountered. The resulting output would look like this:

```
line 04
line 05
line 06
```

Extract control markers are comprised of a three-character sequence that always begins in column 1. The first character is always a comma, the second character is user-defined; and the third must be either an s or an e. In the following table the "f" represents the user-defined character:

Marker Sequence	Meaning
,fs	Start-of-extraction marker
,fe	End-of-extraction marker

When you invoke EXTRACT.EXE, one of the parameters you may specify is the user-defined character. You may wish to standardize all of your files to use markers with the same user-defined letter for simplicity. For now, assume that f will always be used. Different characters could be used to cause different comment blocks to be extracted from the same file for different purposes.

There is one more metastring that EXTRACT.EXE recognizes: the $. string. Whenever this special character sequence is encountered within a line being extracted, the filename and extension of the module being scanned are written to the output file in its place.

This provides a way to have the source filename of a block of extracted text embedded within your documentation when it is placed in the common output file. If you rename a file, you don't have to remember to edit each comment block that may contain the filename. The $. metastring may be placed in any position within a comment line, not just in the first column as with the ,fs and ,fe marker strings.

PROGRAM SUMMARY COMMENT BLOCKS

Since one of this book's goals is to make it easier for you to develop tools quickly, some attention should be given to making a growing collection of them easy to manage. One good way to do this is to place an extractable comment block at the top of each tool's source code module that summarizes the purpose and operating characteristics of the tool. Examples are shown below for the assembler and C cases, with the only difference being the way that a comment block is delimited.

For the assembler case:

```
comment ^
,fs

$.
    An explanation would be written here to describe the
    overall function of the source-code module.
,fe
    =========================================================  ^
```

For the C case:

```
/*
,fs

$.
     An explanation....
,fe
=========================================================== */
```

Once each of your program's source code files is set up with this type of header, processing them with `EXTRACT.EXE` will net you a master index file. Whenever you need to locate a module but can't remember which cryptic eight-character filename you assigned, you can browse through your master index, scanning the descriptions or searching for likely keywords. Note how the `$.` metastring is used to cause the source filename to be placed in the extracted output.

LIBRARY FUNCTION COMMENT BLOCKS

This book's other goal is to help you generate libraries of reusable functions. As above, a key part of that undertaking is being able to find what you want when you want it. The way to do this is through the use of extractable function blocks at the head of each function.

In the following examples, for assembler and C, you'll notice that each line starts with a semicolon. In assembler, this is already a comment delimiter; in C, the `/*` and `*/` comment delimiters are used. The `EXTRACT.EXE` utility can be directed to expect a semicolon in front of the start-of-extract and end-of-extract markers to accommodate this convention. Stock copies of these function header comment blocks can be found within the `\ZLIB\WORK\STOCK` directory on the Companion Diskette.

For the assembler case:

```
;===========================================================
;,fs
; count_widgets - a function to tally all mature widgets
;
; in:  ds:dx -> the base of the widget data list
;       cx = the # of records in the list
;       bx = the maturity count
;
```

```
; out: dx:ax = the total value of all mature widgets
;
;,fe
;=========================================================
```

For the C case:

```
/*=========================================================
;,fs
; dword count_widgets(w_type *w_base, word w_recs,
; word w_mature)
;
; a function to tally all mature widgets
;
; in:  w_base -> the base of the widget data list
;      w_recs = the # of records in the list
;      w_mature = the maturity count
;
; out: retval = the total value of all mature widgets
;
;,fe
=========================================================*/
```

You may have noticed that each of the library source modules on the Companion Diskette contains this type of function header block. You also might notice that each library source module starts with the three-line marker sequence

```
;,fs
;******** $.
;,fe
```

This marker sequence causes a source module's filename to appear in the output file before each of the function header blocks extracted from that same file. Since EXTRACT.EXE will have to be told to expect a semicolon in front of each extract marker, the ones used at the top of the module must conform.

EXTRACT.EXE—PARAMETERS

The parsing logic used within EXTRACT.EXE is part of the library on the Companion Diskette. This same type of parsing logic may be incorporated into any tools you make using this library.

At minimum, `EXTRACT.EXE` must be supplied with the name of the input file or files to be scanned and the name to use for the output file. Here is a summary of the parameter syntax supported:

```
EXTRACT    srcfname #srcflist ... [options]
EXTRACT    @rspfile
```

The options are as follows:

/d=*fname*	Designate explicit destination filename
/m=*char*	Define marker character (default = h)
/r	Write a record header with source fname, date, and time
/b	Write a bar header for each record
/l	Expect leading semicolon before marker
/s	Strip leading semicolons
/c	Use current directory with filespec for metastring substitution

The file or files to be scanned may be specified in a number of ways. In the following set of examples, a comment appears to the right, describing the parameter method.

```
extract abc.txt                    // a single explicit
                                   // filespec
extract *.asm                      // a single wildcard
                                   // filespec
extract abc.txt def.txt ...        // multiple explicit
                                   // filespecs
extract *.c xyz.asm                // wildcard & explicit
extract #filelist                  // a list of filespecs
extract *.c xyz.asm #filelist      // a mix of the three types
extract @respfile                  // a response file
```

When a filename is given with a leading # symbol, the parameter-parsing logic regards it as the name of a file containing a list of file specifications, each of which can be explicit filenames or contain wildcards. This list file method enables you to be selective about which files are scanned and to order the scanning process. It does, however, create an additional maintenance task, in that you must remember to update your list file whenever you add, delete, or rename a tool in your collection. When all files of a certain type within a given directory are to be scanned, and the file processing order is not important, the use of a wildcard file specification is suggested.

When a leading @ symbol is found, the attached filename is taken as the name of a file in which the parameter line can be found. This parameter line can contain both explicit and wildcard-type file specifications as well as filenames that start with a # character.

A mixture of these specifications can be given, up to the maximum length of the parameter line, and will be processed in left-to-right order. The exception is for the response file case. When a filename starting with a @ character is given, it must be the only parameter. Drive and path components may be included in any specification.

The /d=*filespec* parameter switch is used to declare the name of the file to contain the extracted output text. If a file by this name doesn't exist, one will be created. If one does exist, the newly extracted text will be appended to the end of the file. Here is an example of this parameter's use:

```
EXTRACT *.asm *.c *.pas *.bas /d=index.txt
```

The /m=*char* switch allows you to specify the user-defined marker character, with h being the default if this switch is not given. You may wish to use h for header comments and f for function comments, or to establish your own conventions.

The /r switch causes a header line to be written to the output file before each block of extracted text. This header contains the name of the source filename and the date and time that the extraction process was run.

The /b switch causes a dividing line to be written between records. This line is composed of 72 = characters.

To tell EXTRACT.EXE to expect a semicolon in front of each marker sequence, use the /l switch. Then, if you want these leading semicolons stripped from the copy of the text written to the output file, specify the /s switch.

The /c switch allows you to control the formation of the string written to the output file when the $. metastring is encountered. When /c is specified, a string describing the current drive and directory will be formed and prepended to the filename. This switch's use is appropriate only when the input file specifications used do not already include any drive and directory components.

The reason to have the full drive and directory included in extracted output has to do with automated access. When you are browsing through an index file, reviewing the extracted summaries of each program module or library function, you will sometimes need more information and wish to load the original source file.

If your editor supports macros, develop one that loads a file named by the string currently pointed to by the cursor. You will want each filename string to be in full form, or this macro-based loading process will work only when the current directory is the one containing the file you are interested in.

For users of the Brief editor, here is a macro that you could use:

```
ce_func (...)
{
    string a1;
    int x;

    a1 = trim(read ());
    compress(a1);
    x = index(a1," ");
    if(x) a1 = substr(a1,1,x-1);
    x = index(a1,"\t");
    if(x) a1 = substr(a1,1,x-1);
    edit_file(a1);
}
```

To associate this macro with a keystroke, include a line such as the following within your initials macro:

```
assign_to_key ("<Ctrl-E>","ce_func");
```

Once this is done and the initials macro file is recompiled, all you have to do is load an extracted index file into Brief, locate the information you're interested in, place the cursor at the start of the drive/path/filename string, and press Ctrl-E.

Note that if you specify a full drive, path, and filename to EXTRACT.EXE in the first place, the /c switch is not necessary and, indeed, should not be used. The automated file-load trick will still be possible, though, because the expansion of the $. metastring will be done with the fully formed input specification.

RUNNING EXTRACT.EXE FROM A LIBRARY MAKEFILE

Listing 6.1 shows the simple library makefile from Chapter 5, modified to automate the comment extraction process. Whenever any library module has to be rebuilt by this makefile, a flag file named ZLIB.XXX is deleted. This causes the commands below the main target to be executed. The main target is the line where the filename ZLIB.XXX appears to the left of the :. These commands, in turn, cause EXTRACT.EXE to be run and a fresh copy of the ZLIB.XXX flag file to be written.

```
#==== name substitution macros

libname = \zlib\ztools.lib

# id for "include directory"

id = \zlib

#==== implicit rules

.c.obj:
   bcc -c $&.c
   tlib $(libname) -+$&.obj
   del zlib.xxx

.asm.obj:
   masm /mx /z $&;
   tlib $(libname) -+$&.obj
   del zlib.xxx

#==== cause each rule to be examined

zlib.xxx :  inset.obj   touppr.obj    \
            strcpy.obj  strlen.obj
   genndx
   echo x>zlib.xxx

#==== c dependencies

inset.obj   : inset.c      $(id)\zlib.h
touppr.obj  : touppr.c     $(id)\zlib.h

#==== asm dependencies

strcpy.obj  : strcpy.asm  $(id)\zlib.inc
strlen.obj  : strlen.asm  $(id)\zlib.inc
```

LISTING 6.1 Simple library makefile with extraction

```
if exist zlib.ndx del zlib.ndx
extract #zlib.dat /d=zlib.ndx /b /l /m=f /s /c
```

LISTING 6.2   The GENNDX.BAT batch file

The first line of the main target's command body names the batch file
GENNDX.BAT. This batch file is shown in Listing 6.2. It starts by ensuring that any preexisting index file is deleted. EXTRACT.EXE is designed to
always append data to the end of an existing output file, but this situation
requires a fresh start.

The second line of this batch file invokes the extraction utility, specifying
ZLIB.DAT as a file containing a list of input filenames. This file is shown in
Listing 6.3.

Whenever you add a new module to a library, in addition to adding
its name to the makefile, you must also add it to the ZLIB.DAT file. You
may wish to organize the names in this file into functional groups so that the
information written to the index file will be ordered. To make this grouping
easier to manage, comment lines may be placed within a file list file by starting
the line with a semicolon. For example:

```
; parsing modules
getcmt.c
getddt.c
rspfil.c

; i/o functions
inportb.asm
outprtb.asm

; misc modules
homepth.c
lcenap.asm
lcenab.asm
lcdisap.asm
lcdisab.asm


strlen.asm
strcpy.asm
inset.c
touppr.c
```

LISTING 6.3   The ZLIB.DAT filelist file

CHAPTER 7
User Interfaces

On a character-based console the user can send control information to a software tool in two ways: by specifying parameters on the command line used to invoke the tool or by keypresses while the tool is running. This chapter discusses functions that can be used to accept user input by each method.

COMMAND LINE PARAMETER PARSING

This section examines the design and use of the parameter-parsing functions included in the Companion Library. These functions show how library functions can be made flexible through hook functions. They will also be useful in the construction of numerous software tools.

Many of the features supported by this parsing logic were introduced in the previous chapter, during the discussion of the EXTRACT.EXE documentation management tool. Because of the link order control scheme, this family of library functions can be used within device drivers and TSRs as well as stand-alone C programs and stand-alone assembler programs that are designed to link with C modules.

User-defined recognition functions provide for the verification and conversion of a wide range of parameter types. They can be applied to both fixed and switch-type parameters. The matching of switch parameters can be made case-sensitive or case-insensitive. Optional fixed parameters may be skipped by a double comma.

Fixed-Position Parameters

Fixed parameters may be delimited with either a comma or one or more white-space characters (a space or a tab):

```
xprint src1.txt, src2.txt, src3.txt
xprint src1.txt src2.txt src3.txt
```

It can sometimes be helpful to support optional fixed parameters. As an example, let's consider the case of a cross-reference utility that reads an assembler listing file and can optionally be directed to read the associated .MAP file, producing as output a file containing an analysis of the program's data operations. The syntax model for this utility would be:

```
xref listfile,[mapfile,] outputfile
```

In the case where you did want to specify a .MAP file, you might type the following line to specify that QCHK.LST and QCHK.MAP be processed to produce the file RESULT.XRF.

```
xref qchk,qchk,result
```

For the case where the processing of the .MAP file wasn't desired, you could type

```
xref qchk,,result
```

The skipping of optional fixed parameters is supported by the parsing logic included in the Companion Library.

Multiple File Specifications

In many tools, it is desirable to handle a number of source parameters. The EXTRACT.EXE utility is a prime example, where information gleaned from one or more source files is written to one destination file. Another type of program might process multiple source files and make changes to the same files.

To illustrate this, let's consider the case of a program named CLEANTXT.EXE—a tool that reads each line of a text file, performs certain transformations on its text, and updates those changes back to the original file. As a matter of convenience, we'd like to be able to supply more than one file specification to CLEANTXT. Using the Companion Library's parsing logic, we can easily produce a syntax much like that of the EXTRACT.EXE tool, except that there is no need to specify a destination file:

```
cleantxt abc.txt              // a single explicit
                              // filespec
cleantxt *.asm                // a single wildcard
                              // filespec
```

```
cleantxt abc.txt def.txt ...      // multiple explicit
                                  // filespecs
cleantxt *.c xyz.asm              // wildcard & explicit
cleantxt #filelist                // a list of filespecs
cleantxt *.c xyz.asm #filelist    // a mix of the three
                                  // types
cleantxt @respfile                // a response file
```

A file specification given with a leading # symbol designates a file containing a list of filenames, each of which can be an explicit filename or contain wildcards. A specification starting with a @ symbol designates a response file — where the named file is to be opened and read to obtain the actual parameter line.

Note that neither of these methods should be used when this parsing logic is used from within a device driver's initialization section. DOS doesn't officially support file I/O during device driver initialization.

Through each of these various means, multiple source files can be specified to a utility such as CLEANTXT.EXE. But it is important to note that the processing of wildcard file specifications and files that contain lists of other filenames is not purely a parameter-parsing function, since disk I/O must be done to scan the disk directory and locate each matching file. The next chapter delves into the operation of the file-processing Companion Library functions that work in concert with parsing logic to support this type of situation.

For cases where a destination file must be specified, various possibilities exist. A switch parameter can be used, as is done with EXTRACT.EXE:

```
extract /d=index.txt src1.txt src2.txt ...
```

Another alternative is to list the destination file specification as the first fixed parameter (a nonswitch parameter). Then any and all remaining nonswitch parameters can be regarded as source file specifications. Following is an example involving an archive utility:

```
archive archv1 srcfile1.c srcfile2.c *.h
```

A variation on the foregoing method would be to regard the last nonswitch parameter as the destination file specification.

Switch Parameters

In the simplest case, a switch parameter can indicate by its very existence that a certain action is to occur. With the EXTRACT.EXE tool, the /b switch is of this type. When it is included on the parameter line, a bar header will be written before each extracted record.

In contrast, the `/d` switch for this same tool includes additional information. Following this switch must be the specification of the file to which the extracted output text is to be written. This must be given in the form `/d=` *fname.*

The parsing functions of the Companion Library contain all logic necessary to validate and record simple switch parameters. To perform this task for nonsimple switch parameters requires that the parsing logic be extensible. The internal parsing process must be augmented through caller-supplied code. This is handled through hook functions.

A function "hooked in" for this purpose is known as a *recognition function.* Several are provided in the Companion Library, and you can write more to extend the set. The supplied set of recognition functions handles the following types of information passed with switch parameters:

- A hex number (for example, `/pb=03BC`)
- A filename (for example, `/d=widgets.txt`)
- A character (for example, `/c=r`)

In most simple tools, the position of the switch within the parameter line is not important—all that matters is whether the switch is included or not. For cases where a switch's position is important, the necessary information is made available by the parsing logic. For example, you could modify **EXTRACT.EXE** to write bar record headers only to extractions taken from files encountered after the `/b` switch. In the following line, the `/b` switch would not apply to any files found through the `c:\docs\*.txt` file specification but would apply to all files found through all subsequent specifications:

```
extract /d=index.txt c:\docs\*.txt /b c:\docs\*.doc
c:\doc2\*.txt
```

PARSTEST.C, located within the directory `\ZLIB\WORK`, provides an example of switch-dependent parameter parsing.

Switch parameters may consist of either one or two characters. Single-character switches are simpler and faster to type, but double-character ones can be easier to remember, since you get more of a chance to build an abbreviation or acronym (for example, `/pa=03f8` where `pa` stands for Port Address). One word of caution, however: It's best to avoid the use of both single- and double-character switches in the same program. If you use a switch `/s` and a switch `/sr`, the parsing logic will become confused, regarding `/s` as an improperly formed `/sr` switch or visa versa.

It is also possible to specify that switch parameter parsing be done with case sensitivity, where a parameter `/r` could carry a different meaning from

The file /R. Further, you can specify whether duplicate occurrences of the same switch should be flagged as an error or allowed. Duplicate switches could be appropriate when position-dependent processing is being done.

Setting Up the Parsing Logic

The basic steps involved in the use of the parsing functions are outlined on pages 121–124. Refer to the example code in Listing 7.1.

```
//======================================================================
//==== parsing definitions, data, and functions

#define SWP_CNT            2      // total # of switch parms
ld_swptype swp_list[SWP_CNT]     // list of recs for switches

#define SW_GENINDEX swp_list[0].state   //  /i
#define SW_AUXFILE  swp_list[1].state   //  /d=fname

#define FXP_CNT 2           // total # of fixed parms
ld_fxptype fxp_list[FXP_CNT]; // list of recs for fixed parms

#define FX_PARM1     fxp_list[0].parm_ptr
#define FX_PARM2     fxp_list[1].parm_ptr

byte parm_line[LD_PBUF_SIZE]   // buffer for copy of parm line
ld_pdtype pdata                // structure for parsing data

  void report_syntax(void)

  lc_disp_str(
  "\n"
  "Parameter rules for XYZ.EXE\n"
  "\n"
  "  XYZ   srcfname dstfname  [options]\n"
  "  XYZ   @rspfile\n"
  "\n"
  "Options:\n"
  " /i         generate index information\n"
  " /d=fname  designate an auxillary file\n"
  )
```

(continued on next page)

LISTING 7.1   Example use of parsing logic

```
word get_d ( ld_pdtype *p, ld_swptype *sw, byte **prs_ptr,
                    word skip_cnt )

p = p
sw = sw
return(lc_getfname ( prs_ptr,d_fname,FNAME_BUFLEN,skip_cnt ) )


byte parse ( void )

ld_swptype *i_sw
ld_fxptype *i_fx;

lc_get_cmtail ( parm_line )      // initialize global parsing data

  if ( lc_rspfile ( parm_line ) != 0 )
  return ( 1 )

pdata.swp_base      = swp_list;
pdata.swp_elements = SWP_CNT;
pdata.fxp_base      = fxp_list;
pdata.fxp_elements = FXP_CNT;
pdata.parm_base     = parm_line;
pdata.csspec        = 0;

i_sw = swp_list
//                    swchar1 swchar2 recog_func no_dup
//                    ------- ------- ---------- ------
lc_swp_assign ( &i_sw,  'I',    0,      NULL,       1      )
lc_swp_assign ( &i_sw,  'D',    0,      &get_d,     1      )

i_fx = fxp_list;
//                    required recog_func
//                    -------- ----------
lc_fxp_assign ( &i_fx,    1,      NULL );
lc_fxp_assign ( &i_fx,    1,      NULL );

// parse the parameter line
```

(continued on next page)

LISTING 7.1   *(Continued)*

```
 ┌─  if ( lc_parse_sw ( &pdata ) !! lc_parse_fx ( &pdata ) )
 │    report_syntax ()
 │    return ( 1 )
 └─
    return ( 0 )
─┘
```

```
//==== end of parsing definitions, data and functions
//=================================================================
```

in the main () function, simply call the parsing ligic:

```
 ┌─  int main ()
 │
 │  ┌─  if (parse () )
 │  │    exit ( 1 )
 │  └─
 │    .... (other main () logic)
 │    ....
 │
 └─  return ( 0 )
```

LISTING 7.1 *(Continued)*

1. Define a macro named swp_cnt to represent the number of switch parameters.
2. Write a data definition for the swp_list[] array. This array of records, which uses the following record structure, must contain one element for each switch parameter. Each data item is an Entry value into the parse engine or a Return value from the parsing logic.

```
 ┌─  struct ld_swptype
 │    byte swchar1           //(Entry)  First switch char
 │    byte swchar2           //(Entry)  Second switch char
 │                           // (optional)
 │    word (*recog_func)()   //(Entry)  ptr to recognition
 │                           // function
 │    word no_dup            //(Entry)  ! = 0 means flag
 │                           // dup as error
 │    word state             //(Return) value of processed
 │                           // parameter
 │    byte *buf_ofs          //(Return) positional
 │                           // sequence data
 └─
```

3. Define a macro name for each switch parameter. Within the swp_list[] array of records, the state field is a flag that is set when the corresponding switch is found within the parameter line. Defining a macro name makes testing this flag field simpler and produces more readable code. Through a #define statement such as those shown in Listing 7.1, you can test for a switch's existence with a statement like if(SW_GENINDEX) rather than having to use something like if(swp_list[0].state).

4. Define a macro name to refer to each switch parameter's position field. This is necessary only when position-dependent switches are to be used. See the PARSTEST.C demonstration program for examples.

5. Define a macro named FXP_CNT to represent the number of fixed parameters.

6. Write a data definition for the fxp_list[] array. This array of records, which uses the record structure shown below, must contain one element for each fixed parameter, which again is an Entry value into the parse engine or a Return value from the parsing logic.

```
struct ld_fxptye
word required            //(Entry)  true if parm is
                         // required
word (*recog_func)()     //(Entry)  ptr to recognition
                         // function
byte *parm_ptr           //(Return) ptr to processed
                         // parameter
byte *buf_ofs            //(Return) positional
                         // sequence data
```

7. Define a macro name for each fixed parameter. Within the fxp_list[] array of records, the parm_ptr field points to the corresponding fixed parameter when it is found within the parameter line. Defining a macro name makes referring to this string field simpler and improves readability. Through a #define statement such as shown in Listing 7.1, you can test for a switch's existence with a statement like strcmp (FX_PARM1,"xyz") rather than having to use something like strcmp(fxp_list[0].parm_ptr,"xyz").

8. Define a macro name to refer to each fixed parameter's position field. This is necessary only when position-dependent switches are to be used. See the PARSTEST.C demonstration program for examples.

9. Write a data definition for a global buffer named `parm_line`, used to hold a local copy of the parameter line. This is to be an array of bytes, using the `LD_PBUF_SIZE` term to designate the size.

10. Write a data definition for a global structure named `pdata`, used to pass parameter data to the library parsing functions.

11. Write a function named `report_syntax()`, as shown in Listing 7.1. This function is called when the parsing logic returns an error status.

12. Write any recognition functions needed for your parsing logic. Recognition functions are covered further in this chapter.

13. Write a function named `parse()`, similar to the one shown in Listing 7.1. Variations on this basic model will be necessary for different cases. When this parsing logic is used within a device driver, the `lc_get_ddtail()` function must be called instead of the `lc_get_cmtail()` and the `lc_rspfile()` function must not be called at all. This is already set up within the device driver template files.

14. The next thing to be done is to initialize the fields within the `pdata` record. This record uses the following structure declaration:

```
struct ld_pdtype
    struct swp_type *swp_base   //(Entry)  ptr to switch
                                // parameter list
    word swp_elements           //(Entry)  # of entries
                                // in switch list
    struct fxp_type *fxp_base   //(Entry)  ptr to fixed
                                // parameter list
    word fxp_elements           //(Entry)  # of entries
                                // in fixed list
    byte *parm_base             //(Entry)  ptr to
                                // parameter line
                                // buffer
    word csspec                 //(Entry)  ! = 0 for
                                // case specific
                                // switches
    word total_swp              //(Return) swp matches
                                // found
    word total_fxp              //(Return) fxp matches
                                // found
```

In the next section of `parse()`, one call must be made to the `lc_swp_assign()` function for each switch parameter. The same is true of the `lc_fxp_assign()` function for fixed parameters. Note how these functions have been designed so that their parameters form a table of parsing information. Other differences will be necessary for cases where only switches are used, only fixed parameters, or multiple source file specifications. Calling the main parsing functions is discussed in more detail in the following section.

15. Make a call to the `parse()` function from within `main()` or another appropriate function that is in charge of initialization processes.

Calling the Parsing Logic

There are five cases to be considered when designing the calls that will be used at the end of the `parse()` function:

1. Both switch parameters and fixed parameters exist.
2. Switch parameters exist, but no fixed parameters.
3. There are no switch parameters, but there are fixed ones.
4. There are switch parameters, and multiple source parameters are accepted.
5. There are no switch parameters, but multiple source parameters are accepted.

The calls to handle case #1 are precisely those that are used in Listing 7.1. Due to the internal operation of the parsing functions, it is imperative that the switch-parsing function, `lc_parse_sw()`, be called before the function that handles the fixed parameters, `lc_parse_fx()` (the reason for this will be explained subsequently). As the following example shows, if either of these functions returns a nonzero value, a syntax error has been detected.

```
If ( lc_parse_sw( &pdata ) !! lc_parse_fx( &pdata ) )
report_syntax()
return( 1 )
```

For case #2, where no fixed parameters are expected, you would make a call to the `lc_isempty()` function after calling `lc_parse_sw()`. After all switches have been parsed and processed, they will have been blanked out of the `parm_line` buffer. At this point, no other parameter data should exist within this buffer, so if `lc_isempty()` returns a nonzero return value, an improper syntax was used:

```
  if ( lc_parse_sw( &pdata )  !! lc_isempty( parm_line )
  report_syntax()
  return( 1 )
```

Handling the case where only fixed parameters are used, case #3, is quite simple:

```
  if (lc_parse_fx( &pdata )
  report_syntax()
  return( 1 )
```

Handling cases #4 and #5 requires involvement with a directory-processing function, which is covered in the next chapter. From a parsing perspective, case #4 would require that a call first be made to lc_parse_sw(), as in the following code. Then, for either case, a call to the lc_process_src_parms() function must be made.

```
  if ( lc_parse_sw( &pdata ) )
  report_syntax()
  return( 1 )
```

In each of these five cases, when this parsing logic is being used within the initialization section of a device driver, all uses of the exit() function must be modified. This is taken care of within the template files for device drivers.

Parsing Logic for Switches

The function lc_parse_sw() parses a buffer for switch parameters based on the data in the ld_pdtype structure and the ld_swptype array of records. The pointer to the buffer to be parsed is contained within ld_pdtype.parm_base. The pointer to the array of ld_swptype records is held within ld_pdtype.swp_base. One record must exist within this array for each switch parameter defined.

For switch parameters, the switch's text will be blanked out of the buffer once it has been parsed. Therefore, if more data must be stored about a parameter than simply its existence, a recognition function must be used.

The position of each switch parameter and each fixed parameter is recorded to support position-dependent switches (see PARSTEST.C).

For each defined switch, if the ld_swptype.recog_func pointer is not NULL, the recognition function to which it points will be called to validate the corresponding parameter. If more than just the existence of a switch must be recorded, a recognition function must be used. These functions typically use global variables to record information about the switch parameter they are designed to process.

A recognition function for a switch parameter is called with a pointer to the ld_pdtype structure, a pointer to the parameter's ld_swptype record, the address of the parsing pointer within lc_parse_sw() (which will be pointing to the start of the parameter to be verified), and a skip count. This skip count is the number of character positions to advance the parse pointer to step past the switch character or characters. The prototype for a switch recognition function is as follows:

```
word rcg1(ld_pdtype *pt, ld_swptype *st, byte
**prs_pnt, word skip_cnt)
```

If a recognition function returns a zero, indicating successful verification of the parameter, it must have updated the parse pointer to the first position after the parameter, including any associated data. If a recognition function detects an error, it must return a nonzero value. It is up to the recognition function to report the error. The lc_report_showsw() function may be used, along with the lc_disp_char(), lc_disp_str(), and lc_disp_err_lead() functions.

On a normal return from lc_parse_sw(), the ld_pdtype. total_swp field will be filled in with the number of switch parameters processed. The state flag will be set within each ld_swptype record for which a switch was found. In addition, the ld_swptype.buf_ofs field will hold the relative buffer position of the parameter.

Parsing Logic for Fixed Parameters

The lc_parse_fx() function parses a buffer for fixed parameters based on the data in an ld_pdtype structure and an array of ld_fxptype records. As with the switch parameter case, the pointer to the buffer to be parsed is contained within ld_pdtype.parm_base. The pointer to the array of ld_fxptype records is held within ld_pdtype.fxp_base. One record must exist within this list for each fixed parameter expected, and the declaration order must match the syntactical order of the parameters.

Fixed parameters are tokenized in that leading and trailing delimiters are trimmed off and each term is zero-terminated. A pointer to each fixed parameter is recorded within the parameter data structure so that the parameter may be used at any time during the program's execution.

For each parameter, if the `ld_fxptype.recog_func` pointer is not NULL, the function it points to will be called to validate the corresponding parameter. Such functions can be made to store converted values in global variables. A recognition function for a fixed parameter is called with a pointer to the `ld_pdtype` structure, a pointer to the parameter's `ld_fxptype` record, and the address of the parsing pointer within `lc_parse_fx()` (which will be pointing to the start of the parameter to be verified). A sample prototype would be as follows:

```
word rcg1(ld_pdtype *pt, ld_fxptype *ft, byte **prs_pnt)
```

If a recognition function returns a zero to indicate successful verification of the parameter, it must have updated the parse pointer to the first location after the parameter. If a recognition function detects an error, it must return a nonzero value. It is up to the recognition function to report the error. The `lc_report_showsw()` function may be used, along with the `lc_disp_char()`, `lc_disp_str()`, and `lc_disp_err_lead()` functions.

On a normal return from `lc_parse_fx()`, the `ld_pdtype.total_fxp` field will be filled in with the number of fixed parameters processed. Each `ld_fxptype.parm_ptr` field will point to the corresponding parameter (isolated by a zero terminator), and each `ld_fxptype.buf_ofs` field will hold the relative buffer position of the parameter, which is useful in correlating the positions of switch parameters with those of fixed parameters.

Parameter Defaults

Where parameters are used, it is often important to control the default values a program will assign to switch-controlled features. For example, the `EXTRACT.EXE` tool supports a switch `/m` to allow a user-defined marker character to be defined. When the `/m` switch isn't given in a parameter line, this utility will use the character h by default. While this default value is hard-coded into `EXTRACT.EXE`, methods do exist to provide more flexibility.

A program can be made to initialize default values by reading data from a configuration file or by having data embedded into the binary code module in such a way that it can be changed without recompiling the module. Of these two options, embedding default values into the binary module is the more limited and cumbersome choice. First, binary file I/O is required to update this parameter information. When a signature string must be located to find the parameter data table, a sliding buffer technique may be required to ensure that a string match failure doesn't occur because the string is split across a buffer boundary.

The second problem with embedding defaults in the binary code is that it is not suitable for tools that must operate in a network environment. With only one copy of parameter default data embedded directly within the binary module, it is not possible to customize each user's session. When parameter defaults are changed, they are changed for all users.

Locating parameter default data within a configuration file does require that an additional file I/O operation be performed each time a utility is invoked, but the I/O involved is simpler and more straightforward, since a sliding buffer is not required. Further, network support is easy, since users can specify their own configuration files through a command line parameter or an environment variable.

For the case in which network support is not an issue and you wish to make the task of locating a configuration file more transparent to the user, the home-path technique can be useful. When a program is first loaded into memory for execution, DOS prepares a string, at the end of that program's local copy of the environment, that contains the full drive and path from which the program was loaded.

If you adopt the convention of always searching for configuration files in that home directory, they can be located through this string. The lc_home_path() function in the Companion Library is provided to support this feature. A variation on this method would be first to check for a configuration file within the current directory, and then search the home path only if the search within the current directory fails.

CONSOLE INPUT PROCESSING

All programmers must contend with obtaining and analyzing keyboard input at some point. This section explores a technique for processing console input that incorporates support for a number of features:

1. Keystroke macros
2. Mouse emulation of cursor keys
3. Centralized hot key management, for pop-up windows and related functions
4. A console stack, for animating an application or for prestuffing strings as default choices for prompts
5. Keystroke logging
6. Redefinition of the keyboard

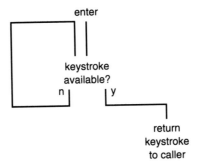

FIGURE 7.1 A simple "hang for a key" function.

7. Execution of background processes—sort a database or print while console input is being waited on
8. Recall of previous command entries

A principal requirement of this technique is that one central, low-level function be used to fetch keystroke data. As seen in Figure 7.1, a getkeys function consists of a simple polling loop. A modified version of this simple model, shown in Figure 7.2, takes advantage of the fact that a significant

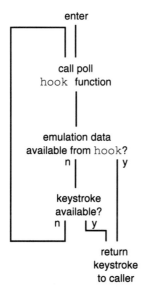

FIGURE 7.2 A function can be hooked into the polling loop.

amount of time is spent in this polling loop—time that can be put to better use.

This second-level model allows emulated keystroke data to be supplied to the caller just as if it had actually been entered at the keyboard. To accomplish this, a poll hook function is called during the polling portion of the getkeys process. This poll hook function call asks the question: "I'm waiting for keystrokes; is any emulated keystroke data available?" In the case of a keystroke macro, the saved list of playback data would be supplied through this interface—one character code per call.

While this second-level model does a fine job of providing for the playback of a macro, how do we detect the macro's activation in the first place? Figure 7.3 shows how another hook function call can be added to the getkeys logic. This new function, known as a *filter hook*, is called each time keystroke data is obtained, either from a poll hook or from keyboard input. When

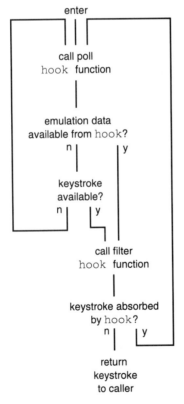

FIGURE 7.3 Adding a call to a filter hook function.

a filter function designed for macro support detects its playback hot key, it signals the corresponding macro poll function to begin supplying keycodes.

Using pointers to functions in this way provides a controlled and defined means of access to the getkeys process. Through this extensible interface, one central getkeys function can be implemented and features added later as needed for each case. The getkeys function can be developed, debugged, documented, incorporated into a library of console input functions, and then forgotten about (from a development standpoint).

The Polling Hook

By making a call to a hook routine during its polling loop, the getkeys function is in effect announcing to the rest of the application that:

1. There is idle time for other processes to be performed, such as background printing or the updating of a real-time display such as a clock.
2. The getkeys function is open for influence.

Fake keystroke data can be supplied to effect macro playback, prestuffing of prompts, mouse emulation, and so on. The call to the polling hook routine must be placed before the test for available data from the actual keyboard. The playback of a macro sequence, or similar emulation process, should supersede keyboard entries, which may be made while a playback is running.

The Filter Hook

When a filter hook call is made, the getkeys logic is, in effect, announcing, "Here is the current keystroke, in case any filter hook processes are interested." Filter hook functions can then analyze the keystroke data and take appropriate action.

Support of hot keys within an application is a typical use for a filter hook function. Hot keys can be used to pop up help windows, printer configuration menus, or other user interfaces that must be available at all times. Recording keystrokes for later playback is also a task for a filter hook function.

A filter function can take four basic types of action when presented with keystroke data:

1. Ignore it
2. Absorb it (for a hot key)
3. Modify it (keyboard redefinition)
4. Record it (for later playback)

Hook Function Interfacing

If a zero value is returned when the getkeys function calls its poll hook function, then the getkeys logic simply continues on in its polling loop, checking the actual keyboard for data. When a poll hook function does return a nonzero value, that return value is regarded as *emulation* data—data to be used in place of actual keyboard data. The polling loop will be exited just as if actual keyboard input had been obtained (see Figure 7.3).

When calling the filter hook, the getkeys function passes it a pointer to the variable holding the current keystroke code. Once the filter function has analyzed and processed this keycode, it will return to getkeys with a zero or nonzero indicator. A zero return value tells getkeys to return the keycode to its caller. However, this doesn't mean that the filter function took no action on the keycode. It may have placed a copy of it in a buffer, or it may have overwritten the original keycode with a translated value.

When a filter function determines that the keystroke is a hot key it is watching for, it will instigate the appropriate response at that time. Once this process is complete, this hook function will return a nonzero value to getkeys to indicate that the keystroke should not be returned to the caller of getkeys. In this case, as can be seen in Figure 7.3, the getkeys logic will simply recycle back around to the polling loop.

The Library Functions

The following set of keystroke-processing functions is provided in the Companion Library:

lc_getkey()	A hang-for-a-key type of getkeys function that supports polling and filter hooks
lc_set_phook()	Allows assignment of the poll hook for lc_getkey()
lc_set_fhook()	Allows assignment of the filter hook for lc_getkey()
lc_ifkey()	Supports a passive test of available keystroke data
lc_set_ahook()	Allows assignment of the avail hook for lc_ifkey()
lc_eat_key()	Clears all keystroke data from the type-ahead buffer
lc_getkey_set()	Waits for a keystroke within a specified set

To simplify the management of extended keystrokes, the lc_getkey() function translates these two-byte sequences into a single-byte value. The file

\ZLIB\KEYDEFS.H provides a set of defined names for use with this family of functions. A demonstration of these functions is provided in the file \ZLIB\GETKEYS.C. Listing 7.2 also illustrates this process with a pseudocode model of the lc_getkeys() function.

Macro Peculiarities

When dealing with the support of keystroke macros, one decision which must be made is how to deal with nested macro invocation. In the event that your application only recognizes one macro playback hot key, the situation is simplified. You either ignore a nested invocation attempt, or provide some built-in exit mechanism—or you end up in an endless loop!

When macro nesting is to be supported (for example, where more than one playback hot key exits) there are several alternatives. In order to make this more clear, consider the case where an Alt-A macro is being recorded and that Alt-B is keyed during that recording session. Further, presume that a macro playback list already exists for Alt-B. One choice would be to simply record the Alt-B keystroke during the recording of Alt-A. Two consequences of this approach—which could be considered features or limitations, depending on your viewpoint—are that the Alt-B macro would not be expanded during the creation of the Alt-A macro and that if the Alt-B macro were later changed, the actions of the Alt-A macro would also change.

A second alternative would be to expand the Alt-B macro as soon as it was keyed in during the recording of Alt-A. This would have the effect of freezing the current definition of Alt-B within Alt-A. A third alternative would be to cause the Alt-B macro to be expanded when invoked but only have the Alt-B keystroke be recorded within the Alt-A macro. This could bring the best of both worlds.

Mouse Movement to Cursor Key Emulation

An application can also be adapted to mouse operation through this getkeys technique. Basically, any application that uses the cursor control arrow keys to make menu selections can be brought under mouse control. The movement data from the mouse can be converted into emulated cursor control keyings, and the mouse buttons can be made to emulate common keys such as Return and Escape.

A programmer can write an application that is not initially "mouse-aware" and then add this feature at a later time. This approach also makes it easier to retrofit an existing application with mouse support.

The basic approach is to create a poll hook function that manages one counter for each of the four cursor control arrow keys. The actions of this

```
byte lc_getkey( void )

  byte t

    while ( 1 )
      call the polling hook, assigning the return to t.
        if ( t == 0 )              // if an extended keystroke
          if ( keyboard data available )
            call DOS to get a byte of keystroke data,
            assigning it to t.
              if ( t == 0)           // if an extended keystroke
              call DOS to get the  second byte of the
              extended keystroke,  assigning it to t.
                if ( t < 0x80 )   // translate the keystroke
                t += 0x80
                else
                  if ( t > 0 x 84 )
                  t = 0


          else
          continue                    // stay in polling loop


      call the filter hook,
      passing the address of
      the variable t.
        if ( filter hook's retval -- 0 )
        break


  return( t )
```

LISTING 7.2 A pseudocode model of lc_getkeys()

mouse support poll function fall into two categories. First, the mouse driver will be called through its INT33H interface to determine how far the mouse has been moved since the last call. This information is then translated into a corresponding count of arrow keyings, and this amount is added to the current arrow key counters.

The second portion of this poll hook process involves testing each of these four counters and determining what keycode value, if any, to return to the getkeys process. You may wish to rotate the choice of which counter is tested first to provide a smoother cursor movement.

Specifics of mouse interfacing are beyond the scope of this book. Refer to the *Microsoft Mouse Programmer's Reference* or a similar work for more details.

A Console Stack

A console stack can allow the user to generate scripts, such as a logon script within a communications package. A programmer can also make use of such a feature to make an application prestuff prompts with a default string. A prompt that asks for the name of a file could be presented with the name of the last file that was used already provided, so that all the user has to do is press Return.

Another enhancement would be to make a filter function that emits enough backspaces to delete a prestuffed prompt if the first key pressed is anything other than the Enter key.

This approach can also support animation of an application. A program could be distributed as a demo by simply creating a keystroke sequence for the program to follow. When working with any type of keystroke playback, you will need to be aware of prompts that flush the type-ahead buffer before calling for their actual response.

Executing Multiple Threads

A poll hook function can be designed to perform other operations besides returning emulated keystroke data. During the time an application is waiting on console input, background processing can be done. The maintenance of an on-screen clock display is one example of such a process. Background printing or sorting of database records can also be a very useful feature within an application.

Throughput considerations must be made when designing this type of multithread execution. If, upon every poll hook call, a real-time clock display is updated, slow keyboard response could result. Certainly, there is no need to update the display until the time value actually changes. In addition, displaying time to a one-second resolution is inefficient when minutes would suffice.

Providing support for background printing is a little more involved. When the user invokes your program's "print" function, write the print output to a temporary file. You want a picture of what the document looks like right at that time, since further changes could be made while the printing is going on.

When this file operation is complete, do not close the file. Use an lseek-type function to rewind the read-write pointer back to the start. Then set a global state flag that will tell the poll hook function that file data exists. During subsequent calls to the poll hook function, it will read a portion of data from the file and send it to the printer.

In order to obtain tighter error control, the INT17H BIOS printing functions should be used, rather than making higher-level calls using the standard print handle or opening the LPT or PRN device. In the event that there is a printer error, INT17H will let you detect it before your program is hung waiting for a printer that is off-line. This is done by making a call to function 2 to request printer status before calling function 0 to actually transmit a character to the printer.

Coding for Reentrance

When a filter routine detects its hot key and pops up a help window, it will then need to make a call for console input itself. This will be a recursive call, so the getkeys logic must be designed to be able to be called when in the middle of a previous call. Since getkeys can be reentered, all hook procedures must be designed to accommodate or control reentrance as well.

Such a filter function must maintain a static flag to let recursive entries know that a previous layer is active. You don't want to allow another help window to be popped up on top of the current one.

Dealing with reentrance requires that careful choices be made with respect to the types of variables used. Local variables that must be unique to each layer of a hook function should be stack-based. Also required, of course, are static global variables such as the one just mentioned.

Interactions Between Hook Functions

In many cases there will need to be a fairly tight level of communication between a poll hook function and the corresponding filter function. When using a polling hook with lc_getkey() that provides emulated keystroke data, an avail hook function should be established for use by the lc_ifkey()

function. This avail hook function must provide a nonzero return value any time emulation data is available.

When a macro playback hot key is detected by a filter function, a global flag must be set to cause the poll function to supply keystrokes from the playback buffer. In addition, when a keyboard redefinition is in effect, it must be gated off when playing back a macro, or you could get a translation of a translation (presuming the translation was in effect during the recording).

Also, if you are using macros and mouse emulation, you would want to make macro playback override mouse emulation, just as it does for input from the actual keyboard.

Finally, if you link a prompt-prestuffing function before a macro function, then prestuffed strings could contain keycodes that activate macros.

CHAPTER 8
File and Directory Processing

Tools that locate and process each file within a directory are common, as are ones that traverse a drive's directory tree structure. A prime example is the point-and-pick type of directory-listing utility that lets you copy, delete, and rename files and see them sorted by name, date, size, and so on. Another example is a backup program that shows a drive's directory tree structure, letting you visually select which portions to back up or restore. Many larger-scale applications also incorporate file- and directory-processing logic within their prompts, providing an easy way to select the file or files to be operated on.

This chapter will explore ways to place the common elements of this type of file and directory tree–processing logic into library functions. Chapter 5 referred to this as a *shell* process—a process that involves a situation-specific portion surrounded by a common portion. Finding each file within a directory or each directory on a drive is a common process, and therefore should be developed into a generic and reusable library function. But the action taken on each file or directory found is, by nature, application-specific. As with the parameter-parsing and console input–processing logic examined in Chapter 7, this is a good place to employ hook functions.

While traversing a directory tree and locating files within a directory are certainly important topics, what is done with each file once it is found also deserves attention. After each line or record is read and processed, the three basic file-processing methods differ according to where the results are written:

1. Back to the original file
2. To a unique output file
3. To a common output file or device (implying multiple-source-file data appended to one common output)

The file-processing functions developed in this chapter are designed to serve both as stand-alone functions, called directly by application-specific code, and as hook functions of the directory-processing library modules. Likewise, the directory-processing modules can be called directly, or they can be used as a hook function of the directory tree traversal module. We will first look at each common component individually and then study how they can be interconnected.

FILE PROCESSING

With file processing, it becomes important to differentiate between text and binary files. Operations typically performed by a text-processing tool include:

- Expansion of tabs or compression of spaces to tabs
- Case conversion
- Applying indentation rules
- Reformatting paragraphs
- Print processing—double spacing, page numbering, headers, footers
- Sorting and merging
- Extraction of marked text
- Macro expansion

Typical binary file–processing operations include:

- Record format conversion
- Searching for records that match search criteria
- Sorting and merging of records
- Calculations and report generation

Because the details of processing binary data are highly application-specific, this chapter will use text processing examples. Many of the basic principles apply to both cases.

A line-by-line type of filtering operation is common when working with text files. Here a function such as `fgets()` (C) or `readln` (Pascal) is used to read each line of text from a file into a working buffer, the buffer's contents are processed, and then the buffer is written to an output file or

```
  ┌─ Word process_file( byte *dpstr, byte *fname, byte attr )
  │
  │  byte workbuf[256]
  │  byte fspec[83]
  │
  │  copy the string pointed to by dpstr into the fspec buffer.
  │  concatenate the string pointed to by fname onto fspec.
  │  open the source file for reading, using the string
  │   in the fspec buffer as the filename.
  │  ┌─ if ( error )
  │  │  record/report
  │  │  return( 1 )
  │  └─
  │
  │
  │  // read and process each line of the file
  │
  │  ┌═ while ( not eof for source file )
  │  │  read a line from source file into workbuf.
  │  │  process the contents of workbuf.
  │  │  write workbuf to the common destination file
  │  │   or device (using a file pointer or handle
  │  │   in a global variable).
  │  └═
  │
  │  close the source file.
  │  return( 0 )
  └─
```

LISTING 8.1 Text file processing, common destination

device. This approach would apply for all cases in the foregoing list for text files except that of sorting and merging, where multiple lines must be stored and processed.

Listing 8.1 shows a function named process_file( ) that reads and processes each line of a text file. This function's entry parameters are designed so that it can be used as a work function with the directory-tracing functions that will be introduced later. Therefore, they may seem a bit out of place in this simple example.

The entry parameters are defined as follows:

- dpstr points to a string containing the drive/path portion of the search specification.
- fname points to a string containing the filename and extension of the file to be processed.
- The byte field named attr holds the directory attribute of the file.

The drive/path and filename/extension portions of the file specification are split up for reasons that will become clear later on. The `attr` field will not be used in simpler direct-call cases. It is part of the interface used when this type of function is called from one of the directory-tracing functions.

Regarding exit parameters, a simple approach is used. A return code of 0 indicates success, and a nonzero value indicates a failure. When more information on an error is required by the calling code, it would be best to design a function such as this to store error location and error type data within global variables.

The simpler go/no-go error status return method is better suited for the case where this function is called by another library function that itself may need to report error conditions. When specific error location data is not required at the point of call, you may simply wish to include a statement, directly within this function, that displays an error message string.

To get a better idea of the details involved in implementing this type of function, let's take a look at a version coded in C. This is shown in Listing 8.2.

One thing to note is how the internal file buffers for the source and destination files are increased over the 512-byte default buffer size assigned by `fopen()`. This is done by the Standard C Library function named `setvbuf()`. When a program is reading and writing files on the same disk drive simultaneously, system performance can suffer when small buffers are used due to the extra head movements required. Larger buffers make for smoother and faster operations.

The statements immediately below the call to `fgets()`, where the pointer variable `nptr` is used in conjunction with `strchr()`, are designed to normalize each line read from the source file by removing the ending newline code. As a result, the `workbuf` buffer will always contain a simple ASCIIZ format string, without an ending newline code. Using this convention can simplify text manipulation operations.

In this example, no actual processing is done on each text line before it is written to the destination. See the source code files `EXTRACT.C`, `XPRINT.C`, and `CLEANTXT.C` for examples of working tools that actually perform some meaningful text manipulations on each line. `EXTRACT.EXE` is, of course, the document extraction utility that was introduced in Chapter 6. The `XPRINT.EXE` tool lets you print one or more files where an optional banner can be included and double-spaced output can be specified. `CLEANTXT.EXE` is designed to help you spruce up a text file by converting all text to lower case, trimming off trailing white space, and so on.

Upon inspecting the `CLEANTXT.C` source file, you may notice a basic difference in its `process_file()` function with respect to the models shown in Listings 8.1 and 8.2. Rather than write the processed output to a common destination file, CLEANTXT's file-processing logic creates a

```
#income <stdio.h>
#include <string.h>
#include "c:\zlib\zlib.h"

#define WBUFLEN   256

FILE *dest;               // global file pointer for output

/*===============================================================
;,fs
; word process_file(byte *dpstr, byte *fname, byte attr)
;
; in:   dpstr -> drive/path portion of the search specification
;       fname -> the filename.ext of the found file
;       attr = the attribute of the found file
;
; out:  retval !=0 if error
;
;,fe
===============================================================*/
word process_file( byte *dpstr, byte *fname, byte attr )
{

  FILE *source:            // local file pointer for input
  byte workbuf[WBUFLEN];   // buffer for input text lines
  byte *nptr;              // buffer manipulaton pointer

  // open the source file and set a larger file buffer

  strcpy( workbuf, dpstr );
  strcat( workbuf, fname );
  if ( ( source = fopen( workbuf, "r" ) ) == NULL ) {
    printf("Error opening source file: %s\n", workbuf );
    return( 1 );
  }
if ( setvbuf( source, NULL, _IOFBF, 4096 ) ) {
  printf( "Error buffering source file: %s\n", workbuf );
  return( 1 );
}
```

(continued on next page)

LISTING 8.2   Actual C code for pseudocode in Listing 8.1

```
// read and process each line of the file

fprintf(dest,"==== processing file: %s\n\n",workbuf);
while ( fgets( workbuf, WBUFLEN, source ) != NULL ) {
  nptr = strchr ( workbuf, 0 ) - 1;      // remove ending linefeed
  if ( *nptr == '\n' ) {
    *nptr = 0;
  }

    // !!!! processing code goes here

    fprintf( dest, "%s\n", workbuf );
  }

  fclose( source );
  return( 0 );
}


//=========================== main

int main()
{

  // open the destination file and set a larger file buffer

  if ( ( dest = fopen( "output.txt", "w" ) ) == NULL ) {
    printf( "Error creating output file" );
    return( 1 );
  }
  if ( setvbuf( dest, NULL, _IOFBF, 4096 ) ) {
    printf( "Error buffering output file\n" );
    return( 1 );
  }
```

(continued on next page)

LISTING 8.2   *(Continued)*

```
// process source files

if ( process_file( "c:\\trash\\", "file1.txt", 0 ) ) {
  fclose( dest );
  return( 1 );
}
if ( process_file( "c:\\trash\\", "file2.txt", 0) ) {
  fclose(dst );
  return( 1 );
}

fclose(dest );
return( 0 );
}
```

LISTING 8.2 *(Continued)*

temporary output file for each source file. Once all data for a source file has been read, processed, and written to the temporary file, the original source file is deleted and the temporary is renamed to replace the original.

Listing 8.3 presents the basic file processing model for this case. From the user's point of view, the contents of the source file would appear to have been modified directly within that original source file. Indeed, for cases where a file's contents do not necessitate an increase in the overall size of the file, a process_file() type of function could be made that writes its output directly back to the source file. This method is not used in this book's examples, however, since it will not work for all cases (such as macro expansion).

Let's take a look at how the last few lines of this pseudocode model would be implemented in actual C code:

```
unlink(fspec);
rename(temp_fspec,fname);
```

The fspec buffer contains the full name of the original source file. Once this buffer's contents are used with the unlink() function to delete that original source file, the temporary output file must be renamed to replace it. Just as with DOS's RENAME command, the rename() function requires that the second parameter contain no drive or path components, only a filename. That the target filename is passed into process_file() separately, through the fname pointer, is fortunate.

Additional methods for deriving the destination filename do, of course, exist. See the section entitled "Wildcard Transformations" for more details.

```
word process_file( byte *dpstr, byte *fname, byte attr )

byte workbuf[256]
byte fspec[83]
byte temp_fspec[83]

copy the string pointed to by dpstr into the fspec buffer.
concatenate the string pointed to by fname onto fspec.
open the source file for reading, using the string
 in the fspec buffer as the filename.
   if ( error )
   record/report
   return( 1 )

copy the string pointed to by dpstr into the temp_fspec
 buffer.
concatenate a unique filename onto fspec.
 (a reserved filename to be used for a temporary
 output file)
open the temporary destination file using the string
 in the fspec buffer as the filename.
   if ( error )
   record/report
   return( 1 )

   while ( not eof for source )  // read and process each line
   read a line from source file into workbuf.
   process the contents of workbuf.
   write workbuf to the temporary destination file.

close the soruce file.
close the destination file.
delete the current source file.
rename the temporary destination file
 to replace the original source file.
return( 0 )
```

LISTING 8.3 *Temporary output file ultimately replaces source*

DIRECTORY PROCESSING

Many high-level languages provide functions that let you access each directory entry within a specified subdirectory. Most MS-DOS C compilers provide a pair of functions named something like findfirst() and findnext() to accommodate this need. Assembly language programmers will recognize these services as INT21 functions 4Eh and 4Fh.

As implied by the name, the findfirst() function must be called to fetch the first directory entry within the directory being searched. The primary input parameter is a search specification string. For example, passing the string C:*.BAT would cause findfirst() to search the root directory of the C: drive for the first .BAT file that can be found.

When a successful return status is detected, this function will have recorded a set of statistics on its find within a memory structure where the caller can access it. Included are the filename and extension of the entry found and the entry's attribute (that is, whether it is a subdirectory, a hidden or system file, a volume label, or a normal file). When the directory entry is a file, additional information is available, such as the date and time that the file was last written and the number of bytes allocated to it.

Once the first directory entry has been processed, the findnext() function is called to locate subsequent directory entries based on the original search specification. For each directory search operation, findfirst() is only called once, whereas findnext() is called for all remaining directory entries that are to be found. The findnext() function will return a "no more files" status when no more matching entries can be found for the original search specification.

Listing 8.4 presents a simplified model of a directory-scanning process that uses findfirst() and findnext(). The flag named first controls whether findfirst() or findnext() is called at the top of the while loop. Note that the search specification string and attribute need be specified only to findfirst(). To perform its operations, findnext() uses data from an internal data structure left for it by findfirst().

A search specification does not have to contain wildcard characters. If the string FILE1.TXT is passed to the scan_directory() function in Listing 8.4, and if that file does exist within the current directory (no explicit drive or path data is included in the string), then findfirst() will return a successful status and the directory entry will be processed. On the next iteration through the while loop, the call to findnext() will result in a "no more files" condition, and the function will return to its caller. If FILE1.TXT doesn't exist in the first place, findfirst() will return the "no more files" status.

These directory-scanning functions treat search attribute specifications in an additive manner. For example, designating that subdirectory entries

```
word scan_directory ( byte *search_spec, byte search_attr )

byte first
word retval

first = 1
while ( 1 )
    if ( first == 1 )
    first = 0
    call the findfirst() function, passing in search_spec
     and search_attr, assigning the return status to retval.
    else
    call the findnext() function, assigning the return
     status value to retval.

    if ( retval == 0 )
    process the directory entry found.
    else
        if ( retval indicates no more files )
        break
        else
        report the error.
        return ( 1 )
```

LISTING 8.4   Basic findfirst/findnext calling loop

be included in the search does not locate only subdirectories. Rather, find-
first() and findnext() will return all normal entries along with those
for any subdirectories found within the search directory. Should your situation
require that only a certain type of entry be processed, you must include
filtering tests to skip all entries that don't meet your criteria.

A Directory Search Library Module

As represented by the basic model in Listing 8.4, a directory-scanning loop
is a shell-type process. An application-specific portion, which processes each
directory entry found, is enclosed within a shell of common logic. In order to
craft a library module that encases the common aspects of directory searching,
a call to a hook function will be employed.

The library function we shall construct, named `lc_trace_dir()`, calls a work function (the hook function) for each directory entry found during a search. This work function must be designed to use the following prototype. The name `work_func` is used merely for the sake of this example—any valid function name can be assigned.

```
word work_func( byte *dpstr, byte *fname, byte attr )
```

Three entry parameters are required. First, `dpstr` points to a string describing the drive and path in which the search is being done. Second, `fname` points to a string containing the filename and extension of the directory entry that has been found. Third, the byte field named `attr` holds the directory attribute for the directory entry found.

Not coincidentally, this parameter definition matches the standard interface presented in the previous section for file-processing functions. By linking a file-processing function to `lc_trace_dir()`, it is easy to develop tools that perform a common process to a group of files.

As stated in the previous section, the `attr` entry parameter is superfluous when a file-processing function is called directly. When a file-processing function is hooked in as a work function of `lc_trace_dir()`, a meaningful value is supplied through this entry parameter and may be used within the work function to filter out all directory entries except for a certain type. It will also be necessary if you are building a directory-listing tool in which displaying the attribute of each entry is desired.

The `lc_trace_dir()` function shown in Listing 8.5 is almost identical to the basic model outlined in Listing 8.4. The only differences have to do with manipulations of the function's entry parameters and preparations done to the parameters for the call to the work function.

Regarding entry parameters, this directory search function requires that the drive/path portion of the search specification be passed in separately from the filename/extension portion. The reason for this will be made clear in the section on "Tree Processing," where we will see how `lc_trace_dir()` can be used as a work function of the directory tree traversal function, named `lc_trace_tree()`. But do not misunderstand—`lc_trace_dir()` may be called directly as well as used as a work function by other functions.

In the following function prototype, `dpbuf` is the pointer to the buffer containing the drive/path portion of the search specification. One thing to take careful note of is that the `dpbuf` buffer must contain enough additional storage space for the longest possible filename/extension type of search specification. The additional space requirement at the end of this buffer weighs in at 13 bytes.

```
word lc_trace_dir(byte *dpbuf, fspc_type *fsptr)
```

```
word lc_trace_dir(byte *dpbuf, fspc_type *fsptr )

byte first_flag                 // marks first time through loop
word err_stat                   // retval from findfirst/next

record original endpoint of dpbuf for later restoration.
make sure the string in dpbuf ends with a backslash.
record secondary endpoint of dsspec for later restoration.
concatenate fsptr->search_spec onto dpspec.
first_flag = 1
while ( 1 )   // find each file and call the work function
    if ( first_flag == 1 )
    call the findfirst() function, passing in dpbuf and
      fsptr->search_attr, recording the retval in err_stat.
    restore the string at dpspec to its secondary endpoint.
    first_flag = 0
    else
    call the findnext() function
      recording the error status in err_stat

    if (err_stat != 0 )
        if ( error due to a no-more-files condition )
        break
        else
        restore the string at dpspec to its original endpoint
        return( 2 )


    call the work function with a pointer to dpbuf, a pointer
    to the found filename, and its attribute.
        if ( the work function's return value != 0 )
        restore the string at dpspec to its original endpoint
        return( 4 )


restore the string at dpspec to its original endpoint
return( 0 )
```

LISTING 8.5 The lc_trace_dir() function

The code within `lc_trace_dir()` must concatenate the filename/ extension portion of the search specification onto the end of the drive/ path string in `dpbuf` for a portion of its processing life. On any return from `lc_trace_dir()` the `dpbuf` string is restored to its original entry state.

Because `dpbuf` must contain an additional 13 bytes for internal use by `lc_trace_dir()`, C programmers should realize that while forming a call to this function using a string literal for the drive/path string will compile, a run-time error is guaranteed. Here is an example:

```
retval = lc_trace_dir("c:\\xyz",fsp1)
```

The second entry parameter of `lc_trace_dir()`, named `fsptr`, must point to a structure of the type `fspc_type`. This structure is defined as follows:

```
struct fspc_type
  byte *search_spec          // search specification
  byte search_attr           // search attribute
  word (*work_func)()        // address of work function
```

The `search_spec` field points to the filename/extension portion of the search string. Unlike `dpbuf`, this parameter is treated as read-only. The next field, `search_attr`, is the attribute to be used in the directory search, followed by the address of the work function. The reason for passing this set of parameters into `lc_trace_dir()` through a structure pertains to the use of this function as a work function of `lc_trace_tree()`.

To simplify the parameter setup required when calling `lc_trace_dir()`, a companion function is supplied: `lc_tracdir_prep()`, which accepts a pointer to a "normal" file specification, a pointer to a buffer where the drive/path portion of that "normal" specification should be placed, and a pointer to a buffer where the filename/extension portion is to go.

A C-specific version of this function is shown in Listing 8.6. Passing the string `C:\XYZDIR\FILE22.TXT` would result in the buffer to which the `srcpath` parameter points holding the string `C:\XYZDIR\`. The buffer at `srcfn` would hold `FILE22.TXT`. Passing the string `FILE23.TXT` would result in a `NULL` string at `srcpath` and the string `FILE23.TXT` at `srcfn`.

The Need for List Building

As previously stated, the file-processing logic within `CLEANTXT.EXE` creates a temporary output file for each source file. Once all data for a source file has been read, processed, and written to the temporary file, the original source

```
void lc_tracdir_prep( byte *input_str, byte *srcpath, byte *srcfn )
{
  byte drvstr[MAXDRIVE];
  byte pathstr[MAXDIR];
  byte fnamestr[MAXFILE];
  byte extstr[MAXEXT];

  fnsplit( input_str, drvstr, pathstr, fnamestr, extstr );
  strcpy( srcpath, drvstr );
  strcat( srcpath, pathstr );
  strupr( srcpath );
  strcpy( srcfn, fnamestr );
  strcat( srcfn, extstr );
};
```

LISTING 8.6   Preparing parameters for `lc_trace_dir()`

file is deleted and the temporary is renamed to replace the original. List-ing 8.3 presented the basic file processing model for this case.

When `lc_trace_dir()` is called upon to process a global file specifi-cation, if its work function writes out a new version of each file, a redundant-processing problem may arise due to the allocation of new directory entries. Say, for example, that the following three files exist within a directory:

```
REPORT.JAN
REPORT.FEB
REPORT.MAR
```

When the `REPORT.JAN` file is processed by the work function, the temporary output file that is created will occupy the next available slot in that directory's list of entries. A peek at the directory structure would show the following:

```
REPORT.JAN
REPORT.FEB
REPORT.MAR
$TEMP$.$$$
```

Now, when the processing of `REPORT.JAN` completes, the original version of this source file is deleted and the temporary output file renamed to replace it. At that time, the directory list will look like this:

```
REPORT.FEB
REPORT.MAR
REPORT.JAN
```

Next, the findfirst/findnext logic within lc_trace_dir( ) will locate the REPORT.FEB file, followed by the REPORT.MAR file. After that, a second processing of REPORT.JAN will occur! To prevent this type of redundant processing, an alternate version of lc_trace_dir( ) is included within the Companion Library. This cousin, named lc_trace_dirl( ) starts by calling findfirst( ) and findnext( ) in a loop in which the name of each entry found is recorded in a list. Once all entries have been found, the work function is called for each member of that list. This way, any changes in the directory order that arise due to the actions of the work function will not cause redundant processing to occur.

Why not always use this "safer" version? If the tool you are building contains a work function that builds its own list of the files found in a directory (for example, for sorting purposes), having the directory-tracing function also build a list would mean additional memory allocation and redundant processing.

The basic rule is, "If a work function of lc_trace_dir( ) could change the order of directory entries within the directory being searched, use lc_trace_dirl( ) instead." Note that from here on, all discussions involving the lc_trace_dir( ) function apply equally to lc_trace_dirl( ) unless otherwise specified.

Processing a Series of Source Files

You may have already noticed that tools such as EXTRACT.EXE and CLEANTXT.EXE make use of a library function by the name of lc_process_src_parms( ). This function can be used to process a series of fixed parameters as an alternative to lc_parse_fx( ). Each parameter is expected to be a source file specification and may contain a drive/path component factor, wildcards, or both. See Listing 8.7 for a pseudocode model (the factor LD_PRSCBUF is defined as 80).

A parameter starting with a # character is treated as the name of a file that contains a list of file specifications, each of which may contain a drive/path component, wildcards, or both. This function is basically a calling front end for lc_trace_dir( ) (actually, lc_trace_dirl( ) is used for safety).

To use this function, you must pass it a pointer to a buffer, containing one or more file specifications, and the address of the work function that lc_trace_dir( ) is to call. The parameter string buffer could contain a string such as

```
FILE1.TXT FILE2.TXT E:\XX\F7*.DOC #FILESET
```

This parameter would invoke processing action for each of the first two files named, then for all files that can be found based on the E:\XX\F7*.DOC

```
word lc_process_src_parms( byte *p_line, word (*wrk_fun) () )

byte workbuf[LD_PRSCBUF]   // line buffer for #fname case
byte *tok_ptr              // use with strtok ()
fspc_type ffx              // lc_trace_dirl () entry parm
byte srcpath[81]           // lc_trace_dirl () entry parm
byte srcfn[13]             // lc_trace_dirl () entry parm
word retval                // holds lc_trace_dirl () return value

ffx.work_func = wrk_fun    // prepare the ffx record with the
ffx.search_attr = 0        // work func's address, a search
ffx.search_spec = srcfn    // attribute of 0 and srcfn's address
set tok_ptr to 1st file spec in p_line
while ( tok_ptr != NULL )
    if ( *tok_ptr == '#' )
    open the source file named by the string at tok_ptr+1
        if ( file open error )
        report
        return ( 1 )

        while ( not eof of source )
        read a line from the source file into the workbuf buffer.
        lc_tracdir_prep( workbuf, srcpath, srcfn )
        retval = lc_trace_dirl( srcpath, &ffx )
            if ( retval != 0 )
            return( 1 )


    close the source file
    else
    lc_tracdir_prep( tok_ptr, srcpath, srcfn )
    retval = lc_trace_dirl( srcpath, &ffx )
        if ( retval != 0 )
        return( 1 )


    set tok_ptr to next file spec in p_line

return ( 0 )
```

LISTING 8.7 The lc_process_src_parms() function

search specification, and finally for each file specification contained within the file FILESET.

TREE PROCESSING

The final disk-processing layer to be examined is that of traversing a drive's directory tree structure. As with the tracing of a subdirectory's directory entries, this is also a shell-type process. The action taken for each of a drive's subdirectories is situation-specific, but the surrounding process of locating each subdirectory is common and is, therefore, a prime candidate for inclusion into a library.

The algorithm examined in this section involves the construction of a tree of nodes using doubly linked lists. Once this tree structure has been built, it can be traversed such that a work function is called once for each subdirectory. Alternatively, logic could be written to support random access (for example, where the user views a display of the directory tree and can select a subdirectory using arrow keys).

Three functions are provided for tree processing in the Companion Library and also described in this section. The management of random access is left to the reader, as the selection method would be too application-specific. The functions provided are the following:

lc_build_tree()   Reads a drive's subdirectory structure and builds the tree structure

lc_trace_tree()   Traverses the tree structure, calling a work function for each node

lc_free_tree()   Deallocates all nodes in a tree

The Tree Structure

The record structure of each node is as follows:

```
struct tn_type
byte prvt                 // describes the prev pointer
struct tnode *prev        // ptr to previous node
struct tnode *child       // ptr to child node
struct tnode *next        // ptr to next node
byte name[13]             // the directory name
```

The `prvt` field designates the use being made of the previous-node pointer, `prev`, and will contain one of the following descriptor values:

```
#define DT_PARENT   0
#define DT_SAME     1
#define DT_ROOT     2
```

The `prev` field is a pointer to the previous node in the structure. The inclusion of this back link makes random access possible and also supports traversal of the entire tree without requiring recursion. To have to allocate memory to a tree structure and also reserve memory for the stack requirements of recursion would be too expensive.

The `child` pointer field locates the first child subdirectory of a given directory. The `next` pointer field locates the next subdirectory at the same depth level. The `name` field is designed to hold the specific directory name and extension of each level. An allocation of 13 bytes is used to account for up to eight directory name characters, one byte for a period, up to three bytes for the extension, and one byte for the terminating zero.

To illustrate this tree structure more clearly, consider the case where three subdirectories exist within the root: \SALES, \NOTES, and \BIN. Two child subdirectories exist within \SALES: namely, \SALES\1992 and \SALES\1993. The \NOTES subdirectory is childless, and \BIN contains a child named \BIN\UT.DIR. Figure 8.1 depicts the tree structure that would be used to represent this sample case. The following table shows which nodes are involved in the representation of each directory level within the tree:

```
Directory           Nodes
===============     ==========
C:\                 1
C:\SALES            1, 2
C:\SALES\1992       1, 2, 5
C:\SALES\1993       1, 2, 6
C:\NOTES            1, 3
C:\BIN              1, 4
C:\BIN\UT.DIR       1, 4, 7
```

For tools and applications that would need to store additional information for each node of the tree, it would be best to refrain from adding situation-specific fields to the record structure. For example, when building a disk backup utility, you may need a flag for each subdirectory level to designate whether that directory's files should be included in the backup. Rather than make application-specific changes to library functions and their common header file, it would be wiser to add an auxiliary pointer field to the

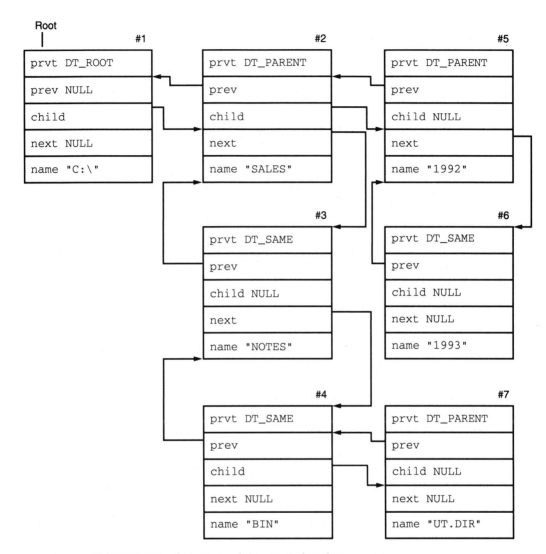

FIGURE 8.1 Structure of the tree of nodes.

node structure—a generic pointer that could be used to locate a record of additional information about each subdirectory level.

The `lc_build_tree()` Function

The `lc_build_tree()` library function is self-contained, in that it does not call a work function. It uses `findfirst()` and `findnext()` with the directory bit set in the search attribute (see Listing 8.8). As each directory entry is located, its attribute is tested for directory status. This is necessary to skip past all nonsubdirectory directory entries such as will exist for normal files, volume labels, and hidden and system files. Note also that the `.` and `..` subdirectories that exist within each subdirectory are not logged into the tree of nodes.

This function requires two entry parameters. First, you must indicate which drive is to be mapped, by passing a drive letter in through the `drvltr` parameter. Second, you must provide the address of a variable that will be used as the root pointer to the tree of nodes. This must be a pointer of the type `tn_type`.

The `lc_trace_tree()` Function

Once a drive's directory structure has been mapped into memory, the `lc_trace_tree()` function can be used to locate each record and call a work function (see Listing 8.9).

Three entry parameters must be passed to `lc_trace_tree()`. The first is a copy of the data in the root pointer—the address of the tree's first node. Second, the address of the work function must be provided, and third, a pointer to an auxiliary record must be passed for use by the work function.

This third parameter is not used internally by `lc_trace_tree()`—it is simply passed through to the work function on each call. Note that the use of this pointer by the work function is not required, but the calling interface does require that a pointer be passed. Pass a `NULL` value if the work function will not need any auxiliary information.

Just as the `lc_trace_dir()` function was designed to call a work function that uses the standard file-processing function interface, `lc_trace_tree()` was designed to call a work function that uses the same interface as `lc_trace_dir()`. This work function's prototype follows, along with that of `lc_trace_dir()`. The name `work_func` is used merely for the sake of this example—any valid function name can be assigned.

```
word work_func(byte *dpbuf, void *pass_three)
word lc_trace_dir(byte *dpbuf, fspc_type *fsptr)
```

```
word lc_build_tree( byte drvltr, tn_type **root_tnode )

byte first1
byte pathbuf[100]

allocate and fill out a tn_type node for root directory.
assign this 1st node's address to *root_tnode.
    if ( error )
    return( 1 )


initialize pathbuf to "?:\" (where ? is the drive letter).
first1 = 1
while ( 1 )
    if ( first1 )
    first1 = 0
    concatenate "*.*" to pathbuf.
    call findfirst, using a directory attribute.
    else
    call findnext


    if ( no error from findfirst/findnext )
        if ( find "." or ".." dirs or if not a dir )
        continue


        allocate, link and fill out a tnode record for the directory.
        if ( error )
        return( 1 )


    else
        if ( error == no more file ) // if no more dirs in current dir.
        determine next node to scan for child directories.
        modify the string in pathbuf accordingly.
        first1 = 1
        else
        return( 2 )
```

LISTING 8.8 The `lc_build_tree()` function

```
word lc_trace_tree( tn_type *root_tnode,
                         word (*work)_func)(), void *passthru )

tn_type *cur_tnode
byte workbuf[100]

cur_tnode = root_tnode
 if ( cur_tnode == NULL )
  return( 0 )

workbuf[0] = 0
 while ( 1 )
  prepare a path string in workbuf corresponding to
   the tree position that cur_tnode points to.
  call work function, passing workbuf and passthru pointer.
   if ( work function has a nonzero return )
    return( 1 )


  // find the next node to process

   if ( cur_tnode->child != NULL ) // if a child exists
    cur_tnode = cur_tnode->child      // go deeper in the tree
   else
    while ( 1 )
     trim the string in workbuf back one stage.
      if ( cur_tnode->next != NULL )
       cur_tnode = cur_tnode->next
       break

     when no more nodes at current depth, backup to
      the parent node of the current level, assigning
      cur_tnode to that parent node
      if ( cur_tnode points to the root node )
       return( 0 )
```

LISTING 8.9 The lc_trace_tree() function

```
 ┌── void lc_free_tree( tn_type *root_tnode )
 │
 │  ┌─ for ( each node in the tree )
 │  │  free the node
 │  └─
 │  return
 └──
```

LISTING 8.10 The `lc_free_tree()` function

To use `lc_trace_dir()` as the work function, simply pass a pointer to a properly filled out `fspc_type` structure as the `passthru` pointer when calling `lc_trace_tree()`. You must also, of course, pass the address of `lc_trace_dir()` to the tree-tracing function through its `work_func` entry parameter.

The `lc_free_tree()` Function

When your program is done processing a drive's directory tree structure, it may call the `lc_free_tree()` function to deallocate the memory used by that structure. The only entry parameter required is the address of the root node (see Listing 8.10).

Interconnections

Due to the interface designs used for hook functions in this family of file- and directory-processing functions, a number of interconnections are possible:

1. Direct call to file-processing function
2. Direct call to `lc_trace_dir()`
   `lc_trace_dir()` hooks to file-processing function
3. Direct call to `lc_trace_tree()`
   `lc_trace_tree()` hooks to `lc_trace_dir()`
   `lc_trace_dir()` hooks to file-processing function
4. Direct call to `lc_trace_tree()`
   `lc_trace_tree()` hooks to self-contained work function
5. Direct call to `lc_trace_tree()`
   `lc_trace_tree()` hooks to custom work function
   Custom work function calls `lc_trace_dir()`
   `lc_trace_dir()` hooks to file-processing function

Case #1 would be used where it is known that a single file will be processed. Case #2 extends the file-processing function's reach to each of the files that can be found based on the directory search specification. Case #3 further extends this processing sweep to include all files matching the search specification within all directories on the drive. The fourth case applies when for each directory on a drive you need to execute some other process than searching through its subdirectory entries.

Case #5 could be useful in a tool that displays the name of each subdirectory and the files within it. The custom work function of `lc_trace_tree()` would display the drive/path string passed to it and then pass that and the `passthru` pointer on to the `lc_trace_dir()` function. The work function of `lc_trace_dir()` would then display the name of each file found. See the file `\ZLIB\WORK\TRACTREE.C` on the Companion Diskette.

WILDCARD-TO-WILDCARD TRANSFORMATIONS

The parsing and file-processing functions of the Companion Library also support wildcard-to-wildcard transformations. You have likely encountered this type of behavior when using DOS's `COPY` and `RENAME` commands. For our purposes, say that you are developing a file transfer utility named `ZCOPY.EXE` and that this tool requires two fixed parameters: a source file specification and a transformation template specification.

Given the following invocation, the intent is that for each file found using the source file specification `C:\*.TXT`, a new target specification is formed using the drive/path component `D:\`, the name of the file found and the file extension `.DOC`.

```
zcopy c:\*.txt d:\*.doc
```

In the following case, each file found using the source specification would be translated into a corresponding target by carrying over source characters based on the ? and * characters given within the template. Finding the file `T1LXX.FIL` would produce the translated filespec `A15XX.FLO` and finding `TPL7.GFX` would produce `AP57.GLO`.

```
zcopy c:\t?l*.* d:\a?5*.?10
```

A pair of functions, named `lc_form_template()` and `lc_trans-late_template()`, is provided in the Companion Library to support this type of processing. See the demonstration programs `\ZLIB\WORK\WILDXFRM.C` and `\ZLIB\WORK\WILDXFR2.C`.

Listings 8.11 and 8.12 present a pseudocode model of the `WILDXFR2.C` sample program. It is designed to accept two parameters, each of which con-

```
main()
fspc_type ffx
byte srcpath[81]
byte srcfn[13]
byte destfn[13]
byte *parm1
byte *parm2

// process the two command line parameters

obtain the first two command line parameters, assigning their
 location to the pointers parm1 and parm2.

// split the parm1 source filespec into srcpath and srcfn.

lc_tracdir_prep( parm1, srcpath, srcfn )

// split the parm2 destination filespec into destpath and destfn.
// (note that the destpath buffer is global).

lc_tracdir_prep( parm2, destpath, destfn )

// derive the reference template from the fname.ext portion of the
// destination filespec string. note that tmplbuf is a
// global variable.

lc_form_template( destfn, tmplbuf )

// prep for and call lc_trace_dir()

ffx.search_spec = srcfn
ffx.search_attr = 0
ffx.work_func = process_file
lc_trace_dir( srcpath, &ffx )
```

LISTING 8.11 Wild-to-wild transform, `main()` function

```
word process_file( byte *dpstr, byte *fname, byte attr )

byte workbuf[256]
byte fspec[83]
byte temp_fspec[83]

// use the template to translate the name found

lc_translate_template( fname, workbuf, tmplbuf )
copy the string pointed to by dpstr into the fspec buffer.
concatenate the string pointed to by fname onto fspec.
open the source file for reading, using the string
 in the fspec buffer as the filename.
   if ( error )
   record/report
   return( 1 )

record the current end point of the string within
 the destpath buffer.
concatenate the string in workbuf onto destpath
open the destination file using the string
 in the destpath buffer as the filename.
   if ( error )
   record/report
   restore destpath
   return( 1 )

restore destpath
   while ( not eof for source )  // read and process each file
   read a line from source file into workbuf.
   process the contents of workbuf (converting to uppercase)
   write workbuf to the temporary destination file.

close the source file.
close the destination file.
return( 0 )
```

LISTING 8.12   Wild-to-wild transform, `process_file()` function

tains wildcards. For each source file found based on the first parameter, a new destination file is created based on the found file's name and the second parameter. The processing action taken for each line of each source file, kept simple for the sake of example, is to convert its text to upper case. In this sample program, the following global variables are used:

```
byte tmplbuf[11]    // reference template
byte destpath[81]   // destination path
```

In the `main()` function (Listing 8.11), the first process of concern is the call to `lc_form_template()`. At this point, the buffer named `destfn` contains just the filename and extension portion of the second parameter, as a result of the call to `lc_tracdir_prep()`.

For the following invocation, the `destfn` buffer would contain the string `x*.doc`. The `lc_form_template()` function takes this string as input and produces the string `X???????DOC` within the `tmplbuf` buffer.

```
wildxfr2 c:\abc\a*.txt d:\xyz\x*.doc
```

For each file that `lc_trace_dir()` can find based on the source file specification, a call will be made to the `process_file()` work function. First among this work function's tasks is to make a call to `lc_translate_template()` using the found filename (in `fname`) and the template (in `tmplbuf`). Given the found filename `"A-FILE1.TXT,"` and the template produced by the foregoing invocation, the result would be formed as follows:

Found name	`A-FILE1 TXT`
Template	`X???????DOC`
	`===========`
Result	`X-FILE1 DOC`

For each character position, if the template contains a literal character, that character is carried forth to the final name. If, however, the template contains the ? character, the character from the found name is carried through to the corresponding position within the final name.

FILTER-STYLE FILE PROCESSING

The last topic we'll visit concerns the implementation of filter-style utilities. This type of tool was first discussed in Chapter 1.

```
while ( fgets( workbuf, WBUFLEN, source ) != NULL ) {
  nptr = strchr( workbuf, 0 ) - 1;     // remove any ending linefeed
  if ( *nptr == '\n' ) {
    *nptr = 0;
  }

  // !!!! processing code goes here

  fprintf( dest, "%s\n", workbuf );
}
```

LISTING 8.13 The file-reading loop from Listing 8.2

While other methods do exist, a simple way to build a filter is to use the same type of file-reading loop as is used in the standard file processing function described in the first section of this chapter. Listing 8.13 contains an excerpt from the C program previously shown in Listing 8.2, and Listing 8.14 shows how this block of code can be modified to form the nucleus of a filter program.

Other peripheral changes would also, of course, be necessary. For example, in a filter-type program, there is no need to open stdin and stdout, but enlarging the buffering used for them is still advantageous. Also, there is no need to close these devices. See the demonstration program \ZLIB\WORK\FILT1.C for a functioning example.

```
while ( fgets( workbuf, WBUFLEN, stdin ) != NULL ) {
  nptr = strchr( workbuf, 0 ) - 1;     // remove any ending linefeed
  if ( *nptr == '\n' ) {
    *nptr = 0;
  }

  // !!!! processing code goes here

  fprintf( stdout, "%s\n", workbuf );
}
```

LISTING 8.14 The nucleus of a filter utility

Appendix A
Pseudocode Conventions

The goal of this section is to establish a generic pseudocode presentation method that will be used throughout the book. The pseudocode method was chosen because it depicts program logic in a language-independent way, yet provides a significant level of detail.

Action charts are used to define the block structure of the programming examples with a graphic clarity. They also contribute to language independence. Were curly braces used to delineate blocking, non-C programmers would be at a disadvantage. Likewise, if the keywords `begin` and `end` were used, non-Pascal programmers would be out of their element.

If you wish to implement the program examples in a block-structured procedural language such as C, Pascal, or a newer form of BASIC, the translation process will be straightforward. Note also that most of the functions described in this book are available on the Companion Diskette, coded in C. A few components are also provided in assembler.

ACTION CHARTS

You may be familiar with formatting utilities that produce a printed listing of a source code module annotated with action chart brackets. By graphically illustrating the nesting and grouping of program statements, these utilities provide you with a picture of a program that is much clearer than the original source code.

To ascertain the logical structure of a C program that uses curly braces and indentation, your eyes must traverse the blank region between the curly braces. When matching braces are dozens of lines apart, this can involve some effort. Following is a small excerpt from a C program:

```
if ( line_count > 1 ) {
  qsort( line_array, line_count, lrec_size, stricmp );
  xptr = &line_array[0][0];
  yptr = xptr + lrec_size;

  for ( x=0; x< ( line_count - 1 ); x++ ) {
    if ( stricmp( xptr, yptr ) == 0 ) {
      *yptr = 0;
      yptr += lrec_size;
    } else {
      do
        xptr += lrec_size;
      while ( *xptr == 0 )
      yptr = xptr + lrec_size;
    }
  }
}
```

Here is the corresponding version of this code where action chart brackets have been applied:

```
┌─ if ( line_count > 1 )
│
│  qsort( line_array, line_count, lrec_size, stricmp );
│  xptr = &line_array[0][0];
│  yptr = xptr + lrec_size;
│
│  ┌─ for ( x=0; x< ( line_count - 1); x++ )
│  │
│  │  ┌─ if ( stricmp( xptr, yptr ) == 0 )
│  │  │
│  │  │  *yptr = 0
│  │  │  yptr += lrec_size;
```

```
    else

      do
      xptr += lrec_size;
      while ( *xptr == 0 )
    yptr = xptr + lrec_size;
```

Through the use of this simple graphic method, a distinct form of confinement is imparted. Whereas the white-space and curly-brace technique leaves the source code statements almost in free float on the page, the action chart brackets provide your eyes with an immediate guide to the logical grouping of the source code statements.

The action chart method has been chosen as the statement-grouping vehicle for this book, not only because of the inherent clarity it brings to source code, but also because it provides a common meeting ground. The curly braces of C and the `begin` and `end` statements of Pascal are all forsaken for this more universal approach.

FUNCTION BRACKETS

Shown below is an action chart bracket that encloses the data declarations and logic statements for a specific function. The function's name appears on the first line. This line will also include information on the function's entry and exit parameters (more about this later).

```
  function name and parameter details

  local data declarations
  ...
  ...

  logic statements
  ...
  ...
```

After the last statement within a bracket is executed, a return to the point of call is implied. An explicit return statement is required only when a certain return value must be passed back to the caller. This topic is also explored later on.

A program's source module is simply a collection of these functions, with one of them being the "main" function, which is executed first.

```
┌── read_source

  open the destination file
  read source file
  close the destination file
└
```

```
┌── process_data
│   process the data in the work buffer
└
```

```
┌── write_dest

  create the destination file
  write the work buffer's contents to the destination file
  close the destination file
└
```

```
┌── main

  call read_source
  call process_data
  call write_dest
└
```

Any module-specific data definitions and global data declarations will appear at the top of the module. In actual practice, each function will also start with a comment header.

LOGIC STATEMENT CONSTRUCTS

Next, we need to define chart constructs for typical logical operations. Shown below is a simple if conditional. The statements within the bracket are executed only when the condition that follows the if keyword results in a true test value.

```
┌─ if ( condition )
│
│  ...
│  (statements executed when the condition is true)
│  ...
└─
```

Here's a more concrete example:

```
┌─ if ( day == friday )
│
│  run payroll calculations
│  print payroll checks
│  print payroll summary report
│  update payroll to general ledger
└─
```

Similar constructs are used for other typical logic statements:

```
┌─ if ( condition )
│
│  ...
├─ else
│
│  ...
└─
```

```
┌═ for ( expression to expression )
│
│  ...
└═
```

```
┌═ while ( condition )
│
│  ...
└═
```

```
┌═ do
│
│  ...
└═ while ( condition )
```

```
┌─ switch ( expression )
│
├─ case value1:
│  ...
│  break
│
├─ case value2:
│  ...
│  break
│
├─ default:
│
└─
```

LEVELS OF DETAIL IN PSEUDOCODE

With the action chart pseudocode representation, three basic levels of detail are possible. The least detailed level is like that shown in the foregoing payroll calculation example. This level could be useful to explain a program's operation to a nonprogrammer, but it is too vague for our purposes.

At the opposite end of the spectrum is the highest-detail approach:

```
┌─ if ( ( source = fopen( file_spec, "r" ) ) == NULL )
│
│  printf( "\n\nError opening source file: %s\n",
│                                        file_spec );
└─ exit( 1 );

┌═ while (feof ( source ) == 0 )
│
│  if ( ( fgets( workbuf, wbuflen, source ) ) == NULL )
│                        break;     !!!! better method??
│  ...
│  (additional processing statements here)
│  ...
└─ fprintf( dest,"%s\n",workbuf );

fclose( source );
```

This is basically full C source code, although action chart brackets are used in place of the curly braces. The same thing could be done with Pascal and its `begin` and `end` statements or for other procedural languages. This book will take a middle approach, with the goal of being less terse than the high-detail version, but more informative than the overview method. With this middle approach, the foregoing source code would be represented as follows:

```
open source file for reading

   ┌─ if ( open error )
   │
   │  display: "Error opening source file"
   │  exit ( 1 )
   └─
   ┌═ while ( not eof source )
   │
   │  read line into workbuf
   │  ...
   │  (additional processing statements here)
   │  ...
   │  write workbuf to destination file
   └═

   close source file
```

Now, non-C programmers may complain that the syntax used is heavily influenced by C, whereas C purists may balk at this watered-down version, calling it pidgin C. Such is the nature of walking a middle path!

Rather than invent a new syntax, much of the syntax of C will be adopted, because it is concise and well defined. However, more English-like descriptions will be substituted in place of the more terse syntax. Further, the convention of one statement per line will always be used, so there is no need for semicolons.

SIMPLE DATA DECLARATIONS

To further support the goal of language independence, variables declared in the programming examples will be limited to simple variables of the following set of data types, as well as structures made up of simple variables of these types. The one exception to this is the case of pointer variables, which are treated in the next section.

byte   Eight-bit; unsigned; used for ASCII characters, state variables, boolean flags, and small counters and array indexes where the 0–255 range is sufficient.

`word`	16-bit; unsigned; range of 0–65535; used for counters, arithmetic processing, and so on.
`dword`	32-bit; unsigned; range of 0–4,297,967,295; use for large counters, arithmetic processing, and far pointers.

When a variable is declared, the form used is *type varname*. For example, the declaration for a variable named `key`, used to hold a character input from the keyboard, would be

```
byte key
```

When reading declarations of this form, it can be useful to apply the template "A *type* type of variable named *varname*." Shown below are a number of declarations where this template has been written as a comment. (Since this book's pseudocode is fairly close to being source code already, comments will be treated as a separate type of text and marked as such using the `//` comment delimiter, introduced with the C++ language.)

```
byte recalc_flag        // a byte type of variable
                        // named recalc_flag

word total_widgets      // a word type of variable
                        // named total_widgets

dword rec_ptr           // a dword type of variable
                        // named rec_ptr
```

As mentioned, declarations made at the top of a source module, outside of any function bracket, are global in scope. Conversely, variables declared within a function are local to that function. In the example that follows, the pointer `list_ptr` can be referenced within any of the functions within this module, whereas the flag `needs_update` is known only within the function `process_list_element()`:

```
┌─ module: updlist
│
│  dword list_ptr          // global pointer to current list
│
│  ┌─ void traverse_list( void )
│  │
│  │  ...
│  │  (statements for this function)
│  │  ...
│  └─
```

```
┌─ byte process_list_element( void )
│
│  byte needs_update     // flag, local in scope
│
│  ...
│  (statements for this function)
│  ...
└─
```

A C-based version of these data declarations is contained within the header file ASMTYPES.H, which is part of the Companion Diskette, and is reproduced here:

```
//==== assembler equivalent storage types

typedef unsigned char byte;
typedef unsigned int word;

#define a_ofs 0
#define a_seg 1
typedef union {
  word h[2];                 // access to each half of the ptr
  byte far *bptr;            // ptr for a byte operation
  word far *wptr;            // ptr for a word operation
  unsigned long far *lptr;   // ptr for a long
  void far *vptr;            // for ptr to ptr copies
  long li;                   // double word numbers
  void far (*ffptrv)();      // ptr to far function
                             // returning void
  word far (*ffptri)();      // ptr to far function
                             // returning word
} dword;

#define SETDWORD(x,s,o) (x).h[a_seg]=s; (x).h[a_ofs]=o
#define DSEG(x) (x).h[a_seg]
#define DOFS(x) (x).h[a_ofs]
```

STRUCTURE DECLARATIONS

The implementation of structure variables will involve two separate syntactical constructs: a definition and one or more declarations. To define a structure is to create a new data type. In the following example, the term following the `struct` keyword is the name of the new data type.

```
struct cache_ele

byte  caDirty
dword caBufferPtr
word  caLastAccessTime
```

By itself, a structure definition does not result in the allocation of a real variable. It only defines the structure that will be used when a variable declaration is made using this new type. Here are two variable declarations using this new `cache_ele` type:

```
cache_ele first
```

```
cache_ele second
```

Applying the template from the previous section would produce the following phrases:

A `cache_ele` type of variable named `first`
A `cache_ele` type of variable named `second`

ARRAYS AND STRINGS

Arrays are declared using the form *type varname* [*elements*]. Some examples would be:

```
byte playing_cards[52]
```

```
word game_points[100]
```

The interpretation template to use here is "An array named *varname* containing *elements* records of type *type*." Applying this to the foregoing examples produces the following:

An array named `playing_cards` containing 52 records of type `byte`
An array named `game_points` containing 100 records of type `word`

As in C, indexing operations involving arrays are always zero-based. In other words, the first element of `playing_cards[]` is element number 0.

This also means that the index of the last element is always one less than the total number of elements.

```
card1 = playing_cards[0]    // read the first element

card52 = playing_cards[51]  // read the last element
```

In this pseudolanguage, arrays will be used to hold not only collections of discrete data items but also character strings. Arrays of type `byte` will always be used where string storage is involved.

Strings are stored in ASCIIZ format, meaning that a binary zero byte is used to mark the end of the string. When sizing an array to hold a string, a sufficient number of bytes will always be declared to hold the maximum string length plus one more byte for the binary zero terminator.

POINTERS AND HEX NUMBERS

A pointer variable holds the address of some location within memory. Nothing more, nothing less. This address might be that of a previously declared variable, the address of some intermediate location within a previously declared variable, the address of a point within a dynamically allocated block of memory (such as a block taken from the heap), or the address of a system-common piece of memory, such as an interrupt vector table entry, or a point within the BIOS data area at absolute address 0040:0000.

Any time an address is listed using four digits, a colon, and then four more digits, this is a hexadecimal representation of a segment:offset type address. Since these digits are of the hexadecimal variety, they may include not only the "normal" digits of 0 through 9 but also the letters A through F.

When an address is listed such as 0040:0000 or 3F02:0100, the use of the hexadecimal numbering system is implied. In the case of simple numeric values, where the colon is not used, the default numbering system is the base-10 decimal system. To specify that a simple numeric constant is a base-16 hexadecimal number, the prefix `0x` will be used. For example:

```
0x083C    // this is hex 083C, or decimal 2108

347       // this is decimal 347
```

Now, to get back to pointers, let's look at how they are declared, so that we can start studying how they are used. The signal used within a declaration to denote that a pointer is being created is the asterisk. The form for this is *type * varname*. The template is "A pointer to type *type*, named *varname*."

Here are some examples along with the corresponding template phrases:

```
byte *char_ptr          // a pointer to type byte
                        // named char_ptr

cache_ele *cur_ele      // a pointer to type cache_ele
                        // named cur_ele

word *card_ptrs[52]     // An array named card_ptrs
                        // containing 52 pointers to
                        // type word
```

To make use of a pointer requires that it be made to contain a useful address. One of the ways this is effected is through the address operator, the & character. Following are declarations for a character string array and a parsing pointer, followed by a statement that assigns the address of the first element within this array to the pointer.

```
byte string_to_parse[81]
byte *parse_ptr

parse_ptr = &string_to_parse[0]
```

This would be read as, "Assign to the pointer parse_ptr the address of element 0 in the array string_to_parse[]." Note that the index used could be any valid value within the declared range of 0 through 80.

Once we have assigned an address to a pointer, making use of the pointer in memory read and write operations again involves the asterisk character as a pointer dereference operator. The first statement below assigns the value in the memory location addressed by parse_ptr to the variable ch1. The second statement writes the literal character T to the point in memory currently addressed by this pointer.

```
ch1 = *parse_ptr

*parse_ptr = 'T'
```

Arithmetic operations are often applied to pointers. When this is done, there is an implied rule that you should keep in mind. Any modification of the address within a pointer will always be performed based on the size of the data type for which the pointer was declared. When a pointer to type word is incremented by one, the address within the pointer is actually adjusted upwards by two. Similarly, when a pointer to a structure is incremented by one, it is actually adjusted to point to the location of the next such structure (presuming adjacency).

For example, if the following array declaration results in the fourth element being located at memory address 0x3340, and each element occupies 7 bytes, the variable `cptr` will initially hold 0x3340 but will be changed to hold 0x3347 after the final statement:

```
cache_ele cache_blks[10]
cache_ele *cptr

cptr = &cache_blks[3]
cptr = cptr + 1
```

Pointers are often used to manage structures that are allocated from dynamic storage. This type of allocation also typically involves the creation of linked lists and trees. Following is a new version of the **cache_ele** structure where a child link pointer has been added:

```
┌─ struct cache_ele
│
│  byte       caDirty
│  dword      caBufferPtr
│  word       caLastAccessTime
│  cache_ele *caNext
└
```

This new pointer, `caNext`, enables a unidirectional linked list to be formed. The introduction of a linked list implies the instantiation of a root pointer variable and an end-of-list pointer value. In the following example, the root to be used is declared. The keyword **NULL** will be used to represent an "unusable" pointer value, which can be used to denote conditions such as the end of a list.

The following section of pseudocode also allocates a series of `cache_ele` type structures and uses the **->** pointer-to-structure operator to access individual fields within each node of the linked list:

```
cache_ele *caRoot              // root of linked list

┌─ byte build_list( void )
│
│  cache_ele *caTemp
│  byte x
│
```

```
caRoot = NULL

for ( x = 1 to total number of cache elements )

    allocate 1 cache_ele structure, address in caTemp

        if ( allocation error )

            display: "Insufficient memory"
            return ( 1 )

    caTemp->caNext = caRoot
    caRoot = caTemp

return ( 0 )
```

Let's have a closer look at this -> operator. Just what does the following statement mean?

```
caTemp->caNext = caRoot
```

In this case, the pointer variable caTemp contains the address of the newly allocated block of memory, which has been sized to hold one copy of the cache_ele type structure. What the -> operator does is allow us to access elements of this structure. The above statements mean "Assign the address within the caRoot pointer to the caNext pointer within the cache_ele structure as pointed to by caTemp."

FUNCTION DECLARATIONS AND RETURN VALUES

Several of the pseudocode examples already presented have included function declarations:

```
void traverse_list( void )

...
```

```
byte process_list_element( void )

...
```

```
 ┌  bye build_list( void )
 │
 │   . . .
 └
```

The first term of a function declaration names the data type of the return value. The second term is, of course, the name of the function.

The void type is used for functions where no return value is generated. A function of this type does not need to end with a return statement. When the point of execution reaches the bottom of the function's bracket, a return to the point of call is implied. It is, however, often the case that a return statement is used at some earlier point within the function:

```
┌  void traverse_list( void )
│
│  ┌═ while ( completed == 0 )
│  │
│  │   . . .
│  │
│  │    ┌  if ( end of list )
│  │    │
│  │    │  return
│  │    └
│  │   . . .
│  └═
└
```

When a function is declared to have a type other than void, a return statement *must* be used, and it must name a variable or specify a constant value that satisfies the type of the function:

```
┌  byte process_list_element( void )
│
│  test the list element
│
│   ┌  if ( list element is available )
│   │
│   │  return( 1 )
│   └
│  return( 0 )
└
```

Often, it is desirable to pass parameters into a function. This is handled in the declaration by naming the type of each parameter, followed by the variable name used to reference that parameter within the function. This naming is done within the parentheses that appear immediately after the function name. When a function does not expect any parameters to be passed in, the void keyword is used.

The following function expects to be passed a byte variable and a word variable:

```
byte validate_user_input( byte b1, word w1 )

...
```

The next example shows three things: how a call is made to a function; how the function's return value can be used anywhere a variable of that same type could be used; and how variables and constants are passed into a function as parameters:

```
if ( validate_user_input( data1, 5022 ) != 0 )

display: "Invalid data"
exit( 1 )
```

Another way functions are commonly used is to assign their return value directly to a variable:

```
status = validate_user_input( data1, data2 )
```

OPERATORS AND READABILITY

The primary goal with using pseudocode is clarity, but with the C language it is possible to write code that is quite obscure. Such practices will be avoided in the application of C's operators and syntax to the pseudocode of this book. For example, the use of the ! character to indicate the negation of a logical test is not very readable—not intuitive. Rather than a statement like while (!(eof source)), the more readable form while (not eof source) is used.

Following is a list of the operators that will be used in this book's pseudocode.

Assignment

=	Assignment

Equality

==	Equality
!=	Inequality
<	Less than
>	Greater than
<=	Less than or equal to
>=	Greater than or equal to

Arithmetic

+	Addition
-	Subtraction
*	Multiplication
/	Division
+=	Addition and assignment (for example, x += 5 is the same as x = x + 5)
-=	Subtraction and assignment (for example, x -= 5 is the same as x = x - 5)
*=	Multiplication and assignment (for example, x *= 5 is the same as x = x * 5)
/=	Division and assignment (for example, x /= 5 is the same as x = x / 5)
++	Increment
--	Decrement

Bitwise

<<	Bitwise shift left
>>	Bitwise shift right
&	Bitwise AND
¦	Bitwise OR
^	Bitwise XOR
&=	Bitwise AND and assignment (for example, x &= 5 is the same as x = x & 5)
¦=	Bitwise OR and assignment (for example, x ¦= 5 is the same as x = x ¦ 5)

^=   Bitwise XOR and assignment (for
                          example, x ^= 5 is the same as
                          x = x ^ 5)

Logical

&&   Logical AND
¦¦   Logical OR

Pointer

&   Address of
->   Pointer to structure
*   Dereference

Structure Member Derefrence

*   Associates a structure variable and
                          structure element

Some examples are in order to flesh out these operators:

x++	means to increment x by 1 unit of type x
y--	means to decrement y by 1 unit of type y
s = t << 4	means to shift the value within t four places to the left and assign the result to the variable s
s = t & 0x80	means to derive the result of a bitwise ANDing of the variable t and the hexadecimal constant 0x80 and assign the result to the variable s
t ¦= 0x74	means to perform a bitwise ORing of the value within the variable t

if(x == 1 && y == 2)   means to execute the
...   conditional statements only if
                          x == 1 AND y == 2.

if(x >= 1 ¦¦ y != 2)   means to execute the
...   conditional statements if
                          x >= 1 OR y != 2 (y is not
                          equal to 2).

```
first.caDirty = 1
```
means to assign the constant 1 to the `caDirty` flag byte within the (`cache_ele`) structure variable named `first`

In the name of clarity, the ++ and -- operators will not be used in dense packing, as they often are in C. In this book, they will always be used on a separate line. For example, in C, you could write the following to mean "Read the character currently pointed to by the pointer `char_ptr`, assign it to the variable `data_char`, and then advance `char_ptr` to point to the next character position in memory":

```
data_char = *(char_ptr++)
```

Instead of this dense form, the following more readable form will be used:

```
data_char = *char_ptr
char_ptr++
```

The conditional operator of C will also not be used, as it can make for difficult reading. For cases where the conditional operator could be used, an equivalent `if`, `else` statement will be used instead. For example, rather than use

```
retval = ( input_byte == eol_value ? 1 : 0 )
```

the following form would be used:

```
  if ( input_byte == eol_value )

  retval = 1
  else

  retval = 0
```

Another statement where the syntax will be much more relaxed than the C standard is the `for` statement. For example, rather than use the more terse

```
  for ( x = 0; x <= total_widgets; x++ )

  ...
```

this book will use the following more readable form. Note that when no mention is made to the contrary, it is assumed that the iteration control variable is incremented by 1 each time.

```
for ( x = 0 to total_widgets )

    ...
```

CONTROLLING EXECUTION FLOW

Some action chart methods use arrows to indicate an aberration in the flow of execution. These arrows will not be used here, as it becomes too "busy." Instead, we will use standard C statements to indicate changes in flow: exit, return, break, and continue. We've already met the return statement in a previous section.

The exit statement, shown in several previous examples, causes an immediate termination of the program. It accepts a byte or word value as a parameter, which is then used as the ERRORLEVEL termination value for the program. This is the PC/MS-DOS ERRORLEVEL, which can be tested within a batch file.

The break statement will cause the flow of execution to resume at the next statement below the innermost bracket of the type switch, while, do/while, or for. In the following example, if the line read is found to contain a special stop code, the break statement will execute and cause the iteration of the while statement to terminate:

```
while ( not eof source )

    read line into workbuf

        if ( line contains stop code )

        break

    write workbuf to destination file
```

Where nested for, while, do/while, and switch statements are used, a break statement will cause termination of the statement with the innermost bracket.

Since the break statement plays a major part in the behavior of the switch statement, another example is in order:

```
switch ( get_key() )

  case 'a':
  case 'A':
  function_one()
  break

  case 'b':
  function_two()                    // break omitted on purpose

  case 'c':
  function_three()
  break

  default:
  beep
```

This statement block illustrates again how the return value of a function can be used in place of a memory variable. Within a switch block, a break statement must be used at the end of each case section, or else the flow of execution will continue with the statements within the following case section. In this example, when the b key is pressed and function_two() is called, the design called for function_three() to be called also. For this reason, the break statement was omitted.

Since it is common for a break statement to be used at the end of each case section of a switch block, it is wise to add a comment when this flow-through effect is employed. Note also that with a switch statement it is possible to have more than one case label at the start of a section.

The continue statement is to be used with the iterative-type statements: for, while, and do/while. It causes an immediate branch back to the top of the iterative statement with the innermost bracket enclosing the continue statement.

In the following example, if the return value from the process_widget() function indicates that another call should be made, the continue statement will execute and cause the flow of execution to branch to the top of the do/while loop.

```
  do

   widget_status = process_widget()

      if ( widget_status == retry )

       continue

   widgets_left--;

  while ( widgets_left != 0 )
```

DEFINED CONSTANTS AND RESERVED VARIABLES

To effect a defined constant feature, this book's pseudocode method will again borrow from C:

```
#define term1 term2
```

What this means is that anywhere `term1` appears within a pseudocode example, there is an automatic substitution of `term2`. Let's take a look at a more specific case:

```
#define MAX_CARDS 52
```

```
byte card_status[MAX_CARDS]
```

```
  for ( x = 0 to MAX_CARDS - 1 )
   display: "card #", x+1, " = ", card_status[x]
```

COMMENT HEADERS

At the beginning of each function, a comment header of the following type will be used. Within this header will appear the name of the function and descriptive notes about its purpose, operation, and entry and exit parameters.

```
;==============================================================
;
;
; in:
;
; out:
;
;==============================================================
```

In actual practice, when this comment header is used within a live source file, it will take on a slightly different appearance. For assembler, the semi-colons in the leftmost column already serve the need to identify this block of text as a comment. For C or Pascal, slight modifications are required as shown after the assembler case.

```
;==============================================================
;,fs
;
;
; in:
;
; out:
;
;,fe
;==============================================================
```

Adapted for C:

```
/*============================================================
;,fs
;
;
; in:
;
; out:
;
;,fe
;=========================================================*/
```

Adapted for Pascal:

```
{==========================================================
;,fs
;
;
; in:
;
; out:
;
;,fe
;========================================================== }
```

But what are those extra two lines containing the `,fs` and `,fe`? These special marker lines exist to support the documentation extraction method described more completely within Chapter 6.

TRANSLATION TO ACTUAL CODE

To make use of this book, there is certainly no requirement that you translate each of its pseudocode examples into your working language. You may find that it is enough to study the tool- and library-building techniques presented and begin applying them to your own code. But if you do wish to undertake this conversion, the discussion that follows should be helpful.

Since this pseudocode is so similar to C in the first place, and because a set of equivalence examples was presented in the section named "Levels of Detail in Pseudocode," you will not be labored further with examples of translation to C. Remember also that the Companion Diskette contains ready-to-compile versions of all functions already coded in C.

Let's first see what it's like to translate this pseudocode into Pascal, and then look at a language that isn't constrained by a block structure—assembler.

```
;==========================================================
; void display_tally(void)
;
; in:
;
; out:
;
;==========================================================
```

```
 ┌─  void display_tally(void )
 │
 │   word i
 │   word tally
 │
 │   tally = 1
 │
 │   ┌─  for ( i = 1 to 384 )
 │   │
 │   │   display: "tally = ", value of tally
 │   │   tally += tally
 │   │
 │   └─
 └─
```

Here is the Pascal version:

```
{============================================================
;,fs
; void display_tally(void)
;
; in:
;
; out:
;
;,fe
;============================================================}
procedure display_tally;

var
   i:      integer;
   tally: integer;

begin
   tally := 1;
   for i := 1 to 384 do begin
     Writeln('tally = ',tally);
     tally := tally + tally;
   end;
end.
```

When translating from pseudocode to assembler, note that there is an inverse relationship between the high-level if statement and the resulting assembler code, which will test and jump based on the opposite condition.

The following example should make this clearer:

```
;===============================================================
; word check_version(word minimum_version)
;
; in:  minimum_version = the minimum acceptable dos
;        version # (in normalized form)
;
; out: retval = 1 if current version >= minimum
;        acceptable else retval = 0
;
;===============================================================
```

```
┌─ word check_version( word minimum_version )
│
│  AX = 0x30
│  INT 0x21
│  exchange AH and AL
│
│  ┌─ if ( AX >= minimum_version )
│  │
│  │  return ( 1 )
│  └─
│
│  return ( 0 )
└─
```

The assembler equivalent involves certain decisions regarding parameter-passing methods and the saving and restoring of the working registers. In this case, the entry parameter, minimum_version, is passed in the BX register, and the return parameter word is passed in the AX register. The states of all registers other than those used for exit parameters are preserved.

```
;===============================================================
;,fs
; word check_version(word minimum_version)
;
; in: bx = the minimum acceptable dos version #
;      (in normalized form)
;
; out:ax = 1 if current version >= minimum acceptable
;      else ax = 0
;      all other registers preserved
;
;,fe
;===============================================================
```

```
        assume ds:nothing,es:nothing,ss:nothing
        check_version proc near
                push    bx
                push    cx
                push    bx
                mov     ah,30h
                int     21h
                xchg    ah,al
                pop     bx
                xor     cx,cx
                cmp     ax,bx
                jnae    cv1             ; if ax >= bx, flow through
                mov     cx,1
        cv1:
                mov     ax,cx
                pop     cx
                pop     bx
                ret
        check_version endp
```

Appendix B
C Source Listings

lc_get_cmtail()

```c
#include <dos.h>

#define res 0
#include "\zlib\zlib.h"

/*================================================================
;,fs
; void lc_get_cmtail ( byte *parm_buffer )
;
; The lc_get_cmtail () function derives a unified copy of the
; parameter line by accessing the command line tail in the psp.
; It is presumed that the buffer at parm_line is large enough for
; the worst possible case (128 bytes).
;
; in:    parm_line -> buffer for unified parameter line
;
; out:   none
;
;,fe
================================================================*/
```

```c
void lc_get_cmtail ( byte *parm_buffer)
{

   dword ct_ptr;                   // pointer to command tail
   word ct_len;                    // length of command tail
   word x;                         // misc counter
   byte *xptr;                     // misc ptr

   xptr = parm_buffer;
   ct_ptr.h[a_seg] = _psp;
   ct_ptr.h[a_ofs] = 0x80;
   ct_len = *ct_ptr.bptr;
   ct_ptr.h[a_ofs] = 0x81;
   *( ct_ptr.bptr + ct_len ) = 0;
   while ( lc_inset ( *ct_ptr.bptr, " \t", LD_EXCL_ZERO ) == 0 ) {
     ct_ptr.h[a_ofs]++;
     ct_len--;
   }
   for ( x=0; x< ( ct_len+1 );x++ ) *( xptr + x )
                                         = *( ct_ptr.bptr + x);
   lc_trim_parm ( &xptr );
}
```

lc_get_ddtail()

```
#define res 0
#include "\zlib\zlib.h"

/*================================================================
;,fs
; word lc_get_ddtail ( dword ddparm, byte *buffer, word buflen)
;
; Advance past first term - drive\path\ddname.
; Then xfer to specified buffer as long as enough room.
; Reports error - out of space
;
; in:   ddparm = ptr to device driver parameter line
;       buffer = ptr to buffer for local copy of parameter line
;       buflen = length of buffer
;
; out:  == 0 if no error, else != 0
;
; errs: parameter line longer than buflen
;
;,fe
=================================================================*/
word lc_get_ddtail ( dword ddparm, byte *buffer, word buflen )
{

  word x;

  x = 0;
  while ( lc_inset ( *ddparm.bptr, " \t", LD_INCL_ZERO ) != 0 )
    ddparm.h[a_ofs]++;
  while ( 1 ) {
    if ( x == buflen ) {
      lc_disp_err_lead ( "Parameter line too long" );
      return(1);
    }
    if ( *ddparm.bptr == 13 || *ddparm.bptr == 10 ) {
      buffer[x] = 0;
      return ( 0 );
    }
    buffer[x] = *ddparm.bptr;
    ddparm.h[a_ofs]++;
    x++;
  }
}
```

lc_rspfile()

```
#include <stdio.h>

#define res 0
#include "\zlib\zlib.h"

/*==================================================================
;,fs
; word lc_rspfile ( byte *parm_buffer )
;
; This function supports the use of a response file in place of
; explicit parameters on the command line.  The first and only
; parameter must be a file name which begins with a '@'.  The
; file will be opened and the first line read into the supplied
; buffer.  The maximum line length supported is (ld_pbuf_size - 1)
; characters.  The total buffer size must therefore be
; ld_pbuf_size to account for the terminating zero.
;
; Since successive lines within the file are not read by this
; function, they may be used as comment lines to document the
; purpose of the response file.
;
; in:   parm_line -> buffer for unified parameter line
;
; out:  == 0 if no error, else != 0
;
; errs: the named file cannot be found
;         (or other file open error)
;
;,fe
===================================================================*/
word lc_rspfile ( byte *parm_buffer ) {

   FILE *source;
   byte *tptr;
   byte *xptr;
```

```
        tptr = parm_buffer;
        while ( *tptr == ' ' || *tptr == '\t' ) tptr++;
        if ( *tptr == '@' ) {
          tptr++;
          xptr = tptr;
          while ( *xptr != 0 && *xptr != ' ' && *xptr != '\t' ) xptr++;
          *xptr = 0;
          if ( ( source = fopen ( tptr,"r" ) ) == NULL ) {
            lc_disp_err_lead ( "Opening source file: " );
            lc_disp_str ( tptr );
            lc_disp_str ( "\n" );
            return ( 1 );
          }
          *parm_buffer = 0;
          fgets ( parm_buffer, ld_pbuf_size - 1, source );

          // truncate off the linefeed

          *( parm_buffer + strlen ( parm_buffer ) - 1 ) = 0;
          fclose ( source );
        }
        return ( 0 );
      }
```

```
lc_parse_sw()

#define res 0
#include "\zlib\zlib.h"

/*=================================================================
;,fs
; word lc_parse_sw ( ld_pdtype *p )
;
; lc_parse_sw () parses a buffer for switch parameters based on
; the data in a ld_pdtype structure and a list of records of the
; type ld_swptype.  The pointer to the buffer to be parsed is
; contained within ld_pdtype.parm_base.  The pointer to the
; linked list of parameter records (ld_swptype records) is held
; within ld_pdtype.swp_base.  One record should exist within this
; list for each switch parameter that might be encountered.
;
; For each parameter, if the ld_swptype.recog_func pointer !=
; NULL, the function it points to will be called to validate the
; corresponding parameter.  Such functions can be made to store
; converted values in global variables. If more than just the
; existence of a switch must be recorded, a recognition function
; must be used.
;
; A recognition function for a switch parameter is called with a
; pointer to the ld_pdtype structure, a pointer to the
; parameter's ld_swptype record, the address of the parsing
; pointer within lc_parse_sw () (which will be pointing to the
; start of the parameter to be verified), and a skip count. This
; skip count is the number of character positions to advance the
; parse pointer to step past the switch character or characters.
; A sample prototype would be:
;
; word rcg1 ( ld_pdtype *pt, ld_swptype *st, byte **prs_pnt, word
;             skip_cnt )
;
; If a recognition function returns a 0, indicating successful
; verification of the parameter, it must have updated the parse
; pointer to the first location after the parameter, including
; any associated data.  When a recognition function is not being
; used, lc_parse_sw () advances the parse pointer.
;
```

```
; If a recognition function detects an error, it must return a
; !=0 value.  It is up to the recognition function to report the
; error.  The lc_report_showsw() function may be used, along with
; the lc_disp_????() series of functions.
;
; On a normal return from lc_parse_sw (), the ld_pdtype.total_swp
; field will be filled in with the number of switch parameters
; processed.  The state flag will be set within each ld_swptype
; record for which a switch was found. In addition, the
; ld_swptype.buf_ofs field will hold the relative buffer position
; of the parameter.
;
; in:   p -> a filled out ld_pdtype data structure
;
; out:  == 0 if no error, else != 0
;
; errs: a recognition function returns a !=0 value
;       a duplicate switch is found and its nodup flag is set
;       a switch isn't properly delimited
;          (no recognition function)
;       no matching ld_swptype record can be found for a switch
;
;,fe
=================================================================*/
word lc_parse_sw ( ld_pdtype *p )
{

   ld_swptype *swp_ptr;    // indexes the switch parameter list
   byte *parse_pnt;        // parses the parameter line
   byte *parm_start;       // holds parse_pnt for buf_ofs
   byte tchar1;            // holds the 1st switch character
   byte tchar2;            // holds the 2nd switch character
   byte ochar0;            // holds the actual switch character
   byte ochar1;            // holds the 1st switch character
   byte ochar2;            // holds the 2nd switch character
   byte *tptr;             // used to blank out a switch parameter
   word match;             // describes the switch match
   word se_cnt;            // counts swp_list entries processed

   if ( p->swp_elements  == 0 ) return ( 0 );
   p->total_swp = 0;
   parse_pnt = p->parm_base;
```

```
swp_ptr = p->swp_base;
for ( se_cnt = 0;se_cnt < p->swp_elements; se_cnt++, swp_ptr++) {
  swp_ptr->state = 0;
}

// this loop's purpose is to process each switch parameter

while ( 1 ) {
  while ( lc_inset ( *parse_pnt, " ,\t", LD_EXCL_ZERO ) == 0)
    parse_pnt++;
  if ( *parse_pnt == 0 ) break;

  // check each switch found against each swp_list
  // entry for a match.

  if ( lc_inset ( *parse_pnt, "-/", LD_EXCL_ZERO ) == 0 ) {
    parm_start = parse_pnt;
    ochar0 = *parse_pnt;
    tchar1 = ochar1 = *( parse_pnt + 1 );
    tchar2 = ochar2 = *( parse_pnt + 2 );
    if ( p->csspec == 0 ) {
      tchar1 = lc_toupper ( tchar1 );
      tchar2 = lc_toupper ( tchar2 );
    }

    // This loop's purpose is to check the switch found against
    // each swp list entry until a match is found or all
    // elements have been checked.

    se_cnt = 0;
    swp_ptr = p->swp_base;
    while ( 1 ) {

      // if the first character of the switch matches swchar1,
      // tentatively set match to 1.

      match = 0;
      if ( tchar1 == swp_ptr->swchar1 ) {
        match = 1;

        // If swchar2 is nonzero and if the second character of
        // the switch matches it, set match = 2.  Otherwise,
```

```
    // must reset match to 0 since the entire switch
    // didn't match.

    if ( swp_ptr->swchar2 != 0 ) {
      if ( tchar2 == swp_ptr->swchar2 )  {
        match = 2;
      }
      else {
        match = 0;
      } else {
        ochar2 = ' ';         // blank out for error reporting
      }
  }


if ( match ) {

    // Go ahead and set up the showsw field here.  The
    // no_dup error-testing logic below could need it.
    // Also, if there is a recog_func and it finds an
    // error, showsw must be set up so that the recog_func
    // can simply call lc_report_showsw);

    lc_setup_showsw ( ochar0, ochar1, ochar2 );

    // If duplicates are not allowed for this switch and
    // the state flag is already set, report the error
    // and return.

    if ( swp_ptr->no_dup && swp_ptr->state ) {
      lc_disp_err_lead ( "Duplicate switch parameter: " );
      lc_report_showsw ();
      return ( 1 );
    }

    // When find a match, if a recog_func is registered,
    // call it and presume that it will advance parse_pnt
    // past the parameter (when no error).  Any and all
    // syntax checking and error reporting must
    // be done by the recog_func.
```

```
tptr = parse_pnt;
if ( swp_ptr->recog_func != NULL ) {
  if ( ( *(swp_ptr->recog_func ) ) ( p, swp_ptr,
                          &parse_pnt, (match + 1 ) != 0 )
    return ( 1 );
  } else {

    // When recog_func == NULL, report an error
    // if the switch isn't delimited.  If get past
    // this test, advance the parse pointer just past
    // the switch.

    tchar1 = * (parse_pnt + 1 + match );
    if ( lc_inset ( tchar1, " ,-/\t", LD_INCL_ZERO ) != 0) {
      lc_disp_err_lead(
        "Delimiter must follow switch parameter:" );
      lc_setup_showsw ( ochar0, ochar1, ochar2 );
      lc_report_showsw ();
      return ( 1 );
    }
    parse_pnt++;
    while ( lc_inset ( *parse_pnt, " ,-/\t",
    LD_INCL_ZERO ) != 0 )
      parse_pnt++;
  }

  // Record the parameter as found and then blank the
  // switch parameter out of the buffer to simplify
  // later parsing.

  swp_ptr->state = 1;
  swp_ptr->buf_ofs = parm_start;
  p->total_swp++;
  while ( parse_pnt != tptr ) {
    *tptr = ' ';
    tptr++;
  }
  break;
}

// When don't find a match, advance se_cnt to check the
// next swp_list entry.  If reach end of the list, error.
```

```
        se_cnt++;
        if ( se_cnt == p->swp_elements ) {
          lc_disp_err_lead ( "Invalid switch parameter:" );
          lc_setup_showsw ( ochar0, ochar1, ochar2 );
          lc_report_showsw ();
          return ( 1 );
        }
        swp_ptr++;
      }
    } else {

      // When find a parameter that isn't a switch, must advance
      // the parse pointer to the next parameter.

      while ( lc_inset ( *parse_pnt, " ,-/\t", LD_INCL_ZERO ) != 0 )
          parse_pnt++;
    }
  }
  return ( 0 );
}
```

lc_parse_fx()

```
#define res 0
#include "\zlib\zlib.h"
```

```
/*================================================================
;,fs
; word lc_parse_fx ( ld_pdtype *p )
;
; lc_parse_fx() parses a buffer for fixed parameters based on the
; data in an ld_pdtype structure and a list of records of the type
; ld_fxptype.  The pointer to the buffer to be parsed is
; contained within ld_pdtype.parm_base.  The pointer to the
; linked list of parameter records (ld_fxptype records) is held
; within ld_pdtype.fxp_base.  One record should exist within this
; list for each fixed parameter expected, and the link order must
; match the parameter order.
;
; For each parameter, if the ld_fxptype.recog_func pointer !=
; NULL, the function it points to will be called to validate the
; corresponding parameter.  Such functions can be made to store
; converted values in global variables.
;
; A recognition function for a fixed parameter is called with a
; pointer to the ld_pdtype structure, a pointer to the
; parameter's ld_fxptype record, and the address of the parsing
; pointer within lc_parse_fx() (which will be pointing to the
; start of the parameter to be verified).  A sample prototype
; would be
;
; word rcg1(ld_pdtype *pt, ld_fxptype *ft, byte **prs_pnt)
;
; If a recognition function returns a 0 to indicate successful
; verification of the parameter, it must have updated the parse
; pointer to the first location after the parameter.  When a
; recognition function is not being used, lc_parse_fx() advances
; the parse pointer.
;
```

```
;  If a recognition function detects an error, it must return a !=0
;  value.  It is up to the recognition function to report the
;  error.  The lc_report_showsw() function may be used, along with
;  the lc_disp_????() series of functions.
;
;  On a normal return from lc_parse_fx(), the ld_pdtype.total_fxp
;  field will be filled in with the number of fixed parameters
;  processed. Each ld_fxptype.parm_ptr field will point to the
;  corresponding parameter (isolated by a 0 terminator), and each
;  ld_fxptype.buf_ofs field will hold the relative buffer position
;  of the parameter.  This latter item is useful in correlating
;  the position of switch parameters with fixed parameters.
;
;  in:   p -> a properly filled out ld_pdtype data structure
;
;  out:  != 0 if error, else
;           appropriate entries filled in within the ld_pdtype
;           and ld_fxptype data structures.
;
;  errs: a recognition function returns a != 0
;        extra parameters are found
;        a required parameter is skipped with a ,,
;        or eol is reached first
;
;,fe
================================================================*/
word lc_parse_fx ( ld_pdtype *p )
{

   byte *parse_pnt;              // parses the parameter line
   ld_fxptype *fxp_ptr;         // indexes fixed parameter list
   word x;                       // misc counter
   word cm;                      // comma counter

   if ( p->fxp_elements == 0 ) return ( 0 );
   p->total_fxp = 0;
   fxp_ptr = p->fxp_base;
```

```c
for ( x=0; x < p->fxp_elements; x++, fxp_ptr++ ) {
  fxp_ptr->parm_ptr = NULL;
}
parse_pnt = p->parm_base;
fxp_ptr = p->fxp_base;
cm = 0;
while ( 1 ) {
  while ( lc_inset ( *parse_pnt, " \t", LD_EXCL_ZERO ) == 0 )
    parse_pnt++;
  if ( *parse_pnt == 0 ) break;
  if ( *parse_pnt == ',' ) {
    cm++;
    if ( cm == 1 ) {                // skip (but count) the 1st comma
      parse_pnt++;
      continue;
    } else {
      if ( fxp_ptr->required ) {
        lc_disp_err_lead ( "Required parameter missing\n" );
        return ( 1 );
      }
      fxp_ptr->parm_ptr = parse_pnt;  // record a parameter
      fxp_ptr->buf_ofs = parse_pnt;
    }
  } else {
    fxp_ptr->parm_ptr = parse_pnt;     // record a parameter
    fxp_ptr->buf_ofs = parse_pnt;
    cm = 0;
    if ( fxp_ptr->recog_func != NULL ) {
      if ( ( *( fxp_ptr->recog_func ) ) ( p,fxp_ptr,
                                          &parse_pnt ) != 0)
        return ( 1 );
    } else {
      while ( lc_inset ( *parse_pnt, " ,\t", LD_INCL_ZERO ) != 0 )
        parse_pnt++;
    }
  }
  if ( *parse_pnt != 0 ) {
    if ( *parse_pnt == ',' ) cm++;
    *parse_pnt = 0;
    parse_pnt++;
  }
```

```
      p->total_fxp++;
      if ( p->total_fxp == p->fxp_elements ) break;
      fxp_ptr++;
   }

   while ( lc_inset ( *parse_pnt, " \t", LD_EXCL_ZERO ) == 0 )
      parse_pnt++;
   if ( *parse_pnt != 0 ) {
      lc_disp_err_lead ( "Extra parameters\n" );
      return ( 1 );
   }

   if ( *parse_pnt == 0 && p->total_fxp != p->fxp_elements ) {
      x = p->total_fxp;
      while ( x != p->fxp_elements ) {
         if ( fxp_ptr->required ) {
            lc_disp_err_lead ( "Too few parameters\n" );
            return ( 1 );
         }
         x++;
         fxp_ptr++;
      }
   }
   return ( 0 );
}
```

lc_swp_assign()

```
#define res 0
#include "\zlib\zlib.h"

/*=================================================================
;,fs
; void lc_swp_assign ( ld_swptype **p, byte c1, byte c2,
;                    word (*rfc)(), word nd )
;
; lc_swp_assign () is used to simplify the initialization of the
; switch parameter list - to make it appear in a table format.
;
; in:   p -> a pointer to the switch parameter list
;       c1 = the 1st switch char
;       c2 = the 2nd switch char
;       rfc -> the recognition function  (NULL if none)
;       nd = the no_dup flag setting
;
; out:  none
;
;,fe
=================================================================*/
void lc_swp_assign ( ld_swptype **p, byte c1, byte c2,
  word (*rfc) (), word nd )
{

  (*p)->swchar1 = c1;
  (*p)->swchar2 = c2;
  (*p)->recog_func = rfc;
  (*p)->no_dup = nd;
  (*p)++;
}
```

lc_fxp_assign()

```
#define res 0
#include "\zlib\zlib.h"

/*===================================================================
;,fs
; void lc_fxp_assign ( ld_fxptype **p, word r, word (*rfc) () )
;
; lc_fxp_assign () is used to simplify the initialization of the
; fixed parameter list - to make it appear in a table format.
;
; in:    p -> a pointer to the fixed parameter list
;        r = the required flag setting
;        rfc -> the recognition function  (NULL if none)
;
; out:   none
;
;,fe
===================================================================*/
void lc_fxp_assign ( ld_fxptype **p, word r, word (*rfc) () )
{

  (*p)->required = r;
  (*p)->recog_func = rfc;
  (*p)++;
}
```

lc_isempty()

```
#define res 0
#include "\zlib\zlib.h"

/*==================================================================
;,fs
; word lc_isempty ( byte *test_line )
;
; lc_isempty () tests for an empty buffer.  If the buffer
; addressed by the supplied pointer starts with a 0 or contains
; only white space, this function will return a zero value.
;
; in:   test_line -> buffer to analyze
;
; out:  returns != 0 if the buffer is empty
;
;,fe
===================================================================*/
word lc_isempty ( byte *test_line )
{

  while ( lc_inset ( *test_line, " \t", LD_EXCL_ZERO ) == 0 )
    test_line++;
  return ( *test_line == 0 );
}
```

lc_trim_parm()

```
#define res 0
#include "\zlib\zlib.h"

/*==================================================================
;,fs
; void lc_trim_parm ( byte **xptr )
;
; lc_trim_parm () is used to trim leading and trailing white space.
;
; in:   xptr -> ptr to string
;
; out:  ptr advanced past white space
;          trailing white space truncated
;
;,fe
==================================================================*/
void lc_trim_parm ( byte **xptr )
{

  byte *tptr;
  word string_len;

  while ( lc_inset ( **xptr," \t",LD_EXCL_ZERO ) == 0 ) (*xptr)++;
  if ( **xptr == '\n' ) {
    **xptr = 0;
  }
  if ( **xptr == 0 ) return;
  string_len = 0;
  tptr = *xptr;
  while ( *tptr != 0 ) {
    tptr++;
    string_len++;
    }
  tptr = *xptr + string_len - 1;
  while ( tptr > *xptr ) {
    if ( lc_inset ( *tptr, "\n\t ", LD_EXCL_ZERO ) == 0 )  {
      *tptr = 0;
    } else {
      break;
    }
    tptr--;
  }
}
```

lc_inset()

```
#define res 0
#include "\zlib\zlib.h"

/*=====================================================================
;,fs
; word lc_inset ( byte tc, byte *ts, word if_zero )
;
; lc_inset () tests a character for inclusion within a string. A
; zero return value results if the character is found within the
; string. Since strings must be 0-terminated, a flag is used to
; indicate whether the character is to be tested for 0 or not.
;
; in:   tc = the character to test for inclusion
;       ts -> the set of characters to test tc against
;       if_zero != 0 if tc is to be tested for == 0
;
; out:  == 0 if tc is within the set.  e.g. if tc is within
;       the ts string or if tc == 0 and if_zero != 0
;
;,fe
=====================================================================*/
word lc_inset ( byte tc, byte *ts, word if_zero )
{

  byte *xp;

  if ( if_zero && tc == 0 ) return ( 0 );
  xp = ts;
  while ( *xp != 0 ) {
    if ( tc == *xp ) return ( 0 );
    xp++;
  }
  return ( 1 );
}
```

lc_disp_char(), lc_disp_str(), lc_disp_err_lead()

```c
#include <stdio.h>

#define res 0
#include "\zlib\zlib.h"

/*================================================================
;,fs
; void lc_disp_char ( byte *dchar )
;
; This function provides low-level character display.  Replace
; with an alternate display function when standard
; libraries aren't available.
;
; in:   dchar -> the character to display
;
; out:  none
;
;,fe
================================================================*/
void lc_disp_char ( byte *dchar )
{

  putchar ( *dchar );
}


/*================================================================
;,fs
; void lc_disp_str ( byte *dchar )
;
; This function provides low-level string display.  replace
; with an alternate display function when standard
; libraries aren't available.
;
; in:   dchar -> the string to display
;
; out:  none
;
;,fe
================================================================*/
```

```c
void lc_disp_str ( byte *dchar )
{

  printf ( "%s", dchar );
}


/*================================================================
;,fs
; void lc_disp_err_lead ( byte *dchar )
;
; This function provides low-level string display for error
; messages.  Replace printf() with an alternate display function
; when standard libraries aren't available.
;
; in:   dchar -> the string to display
;
; out:  none
;
;,fe
=================================================================*/
void lc_disp_err_lead ( byte *dchar )
{

  printf ( "\nError - %s", dchar );
}
```

lc_setup_showsw(), lc_report_showsw()

```
#define res 0
#include "\zlib\zlib.h"

static byte *lc_err_showsw = "    \n";

/*================================================================
;,fs
; void lc_setup_showsw ( byte oc0, byte oc1, byte oc2 )
;
; This function is called by lc_parse_sw () to prepare for the use
; of lc_report_showsw ().  If a single-character switch is being
; processed, assign a blank to oc2.
;
; in:   oc0 = the switch signal (e.g. '-' or '/')
;       oc1 = the first switch character
;       oc2 = the second switch character
;
; out:  none
;
;,fe
================================================================*/
void lc_setup_showsw ( byte oc0, byte oc1, byte oc2 )
{

  *( lc_err_showsw + 1) = oc0;
  *( lc_err_showsw + 2) = oc1;
  *( lc_err_showsw + 3) = oc2;
}
```

```
/*================================================================
;,fs
; void lc_report_showsw ()
;
; This function displays the lc_err_showsw string.  It is useful
; for reporting errors within recognition functions.
;
; in:   none
;
; out:  none
;
;,fe
=================================================================*/
void lc_report_showsw ()
{

  lc_disp_str ( lc_err_showsw );
}
```

lc_toupper()

```
#define res 0
#include "\zlib\zlib.h"

/*================================================================
;,fs
; byte lc_toupper(byte t)
;
; lc_toupper() converts the supplied character to its upper-case
; equivalent.
;
; in:   t = the character to be converted
;
; out:  returns the converted character
;
;,fe
================================================================*/
byte lc_toupper ( byte t )
{

   if ( t >= 'a' && t <= 'z' ) return ( t - 32 );
   return ( t );
}
```

lc_getchar()

```
#define res 0
#include "\zlib\zlib.h"

/*===================================================================
;,fs
; word lc_getchar ( byte **parm_ptr, byte *dest_ptr, word skip_cnt )
;
; lc_getchar() is designed to be called by a recognition function
; for a switch parameter.  It processes a switch of the form
;
; /sw=c
;
; in:   parm_ptr -> ptr to parmeter
;       dest_ptr -> destination byte into which char is copied
;       skip_cnt    (passed through from the recog_func call)
;
; out:  == 0 if no error, else != 0
;
; errs: improper syntax in the "=c" term
;
;,fe
=================================================================*/
word lc_getchar ( byte **parm_ptr, byte *dest_ptr, word skip_cnt )
{

  word dest_cnt;

  *parm_ptr += skip_cnt;
  if(**parm_ptr != '=' )  {
    lc_disp_err_lead ( "\"=c\" must follow: " );
    lc_report_showsw ();
    return ( 1 );
  }
```

```
      ( *parm_ptr )++;
      *dest_ptr = **parm_ptr;
      if ( lc_inset ( **parm_ptr, " ,\t/-", LD_INCL_ZERO ) == 0 ) {
        lc_disp_err_lead ( "\"=c\" must follow: " );
        lc_report_showsw ();
        return ( 1 );
      }
      ( *parm_ptr )++;
      if ( lc_inset ( **parm_ptr, " ,\t/-", LD_INCL_ZERO ) != 0 ) {
        lc_disp_err_lead ( "Delimiter must follow char after: " );
        lc_report_showsw ();
        return ( 1 );
      }
      return ( 0 );
   }
```

lc_getfname()

```
#define res 0
#include "\zlib\zlib.h"

/*=====================================================================
;,fs
; word lc_getfname ( byte **parm_ptr, byte *dest_ptr, word dest_max,
;                    word skip_cnt )
;
;
; lc_getfname () is designed to be called by a recognition
; function for a switch parameter.  It processes a switch of the
; form
;
; /sw=fname.ext
;
; in:   parm_ptr -> ptr to parameter
;       dest_ptr -> buffer into which filespec is copied
;       dest_max =  total length of dest buffer
;                     (including byte for terminating 0)
;       skip_cnt    (passed through from the recog_func call)
;
; out:  == 0 if no error, else != 0
;
; errs: improper syntax in the "=fname" term
;       the filename is longer than the supplied buffer
;
;,fe
=====================================================================*/
word lc_getfname ( byte **parm_ptr, byte *dest_ptr, word dest_max,
                   word skip_cnt)
{

  word dest_cnt;

  *parm_ptr += skip_cnt;
  if ( **parm_ptr != '=' )  {
    lc_disp_err_lead ( "\"=fname\" must follow: " );
    lc_report_showsw ();
    return ( 1 );
  }
  ( *parm_ptr )++;
  dest_cnt = 2;
```

```
   while ( 1 ) {
     if ( lc_inset ( **parm_ptr, " ,\t/-",
                                     LD_INCL_ZERO ) == 0 ) break;
     if ( dest_cnt > dest_max ) {
       lc_disp_err_lead ( "fname too long for:" );
       lc_report_showsw ();
       return ( 1 );
     }
     *dest_ptr = **parm_ptr;
     dest_ptr++;
     ( *parm_ptr )++;
     dest_cnt++;
   }
   *dest_ptr = 0;
   return ( 0 );
}
```

lc_verify_hex_fx()

```
#define res 0
#include "\zlib\zlib.h"

/*=====================================================================
;,fs
; word lc_verify_hex_fx ( byte **prs_ptr, word maxdig, word *result )
;
; lc_verify_hex_fx () is designed to be called by a recognition
; function for a fixed hex parameter.  The result returned would
; typically be stored in a global variable.  Use a maxdig of four
; for a word and two for a byte.
;
; in:   prs_ptr -> ptr used to parse the parameter line
;       maxdig = the maximum number of hex digits to allow
;       result -> the integer variable to hold the resulting value
;
; out:  == 0 if no error, else != 0
;
;,fe
======================================================================*/
word lc_verify_hex_fx ( byte **prs_ptr, word maxdig, word *result )
{

  word x;
  byte *orig_ptr;

  orig_ptr = *prs_ptr;
  if ( lc_verify_hexstr ( prs_ptr, &x, maxdig, " \t/-",
      ld_incl_zero ) != 0 ) {
    lc_disp_err_lead ( "Invalid hex format: " );
    lc_disp_str ( orig_ptr );
    return ( 1 );
  }
  *result = x;
  return ( 0 );
}
```

lc_verify_hex_sw()

```
#define res 0
#include "\zlib\zlib.h"

/*====================================================================
;,fs
; word lc_verify_hex_sw ( byte **prs_ptr, word skip_cnt, word maxdig,
;                         word *result )
;
; lc_verify_hex_fx () is designed to be called by a recognition
; function for a switch hex parameter.  The result returned would
; typically be stored in a global variable.  Use a maxdig of four
; for a word and two for a byte.  This is for parameters of the
; general form  /sa=03f8.
;
; in:   prs_ptr -> ptr used to parse the parameter line
;       skip_cnt    (passed through from the recog_func call)
;       maxdig = the maximum number of hex digits to allow
;       result -> the integer variable to hold the resulting value
;
; out:  == 0 if no error, else != 0
;
;,fe
=====================================================================*/
word lc_verify_hex_sw ( byte **prs_ptr, word skip_cnt, word maxdig,
                        word *result )
{

  word err_flg;
  word x;
```

```
      err_flg = 0;
      ( *prs_ptr ) += skip_cnt;
      if( **prs_ptr == '=' )  {
        ( *prs_ptr )++;
        if ( lc_verify_hexstr ( prs_ptr, &x, maxdig, " ,\t/-",
           ld_incl_zero ) != 0 )
          err_flg = 1;
      } else {
        err_flg = 1;
      }
      if ( err_flg ) {
        lc_disp_err_lead ( "Invalid hex format:" );
        lc_report_showsw ();
        return ( 1 );
      }
      *result = x;
      return ( 0 );
}
```

lc_verify_hexstr()

```
#define res 0
#include "\zlib\zlib.h"

/*=====================================================================
;,fs
; word lc_verify_hexstr ( byte **vh_ptr, word *retvalue, word maxdig,
;                         byte *termstr, byte zspec )
;
; lc_verify_hex_str () is used by lc_verify_hex_fx () and
; lc_verify_hex_sw () to verify and convert a hexadecimal
; parameter.
;
; in:   vh_ptr -> ptr used to parse the hex string
;       retvalue -> the integer var to hold the resulting value
;       maxdig = the maximum number of hex digits to allow
;       termstr -> string of terminator characters
;       zspec = ld_incl_zero or ld_excl_zero
;        (for termination test)
;
; out:   == 0 if no error, else != 0
;
;,fe
=====================================================================*/
word lc_verify_hexstr ( byte **vh_ptr, word *retvalue, word maxdig,
                        byte *termstr, byte zspec )
{

   word x;
   word value;
   byte t;

   if ( maxdig > 4 ) return ( 1 );
   value = 0;
   x = 0;
```

```
while ( 1 ) {
  t = **vh_ptr;
  if ( lc_inset ( t, termstr, zspec ) == 0 ) break;
  if ( lc_inset ( t, "0123456789abcdefABCDEF",
                                        ld_excl_zero ) == 0 ) {
    ( *vh_ptr )++;
    x++;
    value *= 16;
    if ( lc_inset ( t,"abcdef", ld_excl_zero ) == 0 ) {
      value += ( t - 'a' + 0xa );
    } else {
      if ( lc_inset ( t, "ABCDEF", ld_excl_zero ) == 0 ) {
        value += ( t - 'A' + 0xa );
      } else {
        value += ( t - '0');
      }
    }
  } else {
    return ( 1 );
  }
}
if ( x == 0 || x > maxdig ) return ( 1 );
*retvalue = value;
return ( 0 );
}
```

lc_find_files()

```
#include <alloc.h>
#include <dir.h>
#include <dos.h>
#include <string.h>

#define res 0
#include "\zlib\zlib.h"

/*==================================================================
;,fs
; word lc_find_files ( byte *filespec )
;
; findfirst () and findnext () are used to build a list of target
; files in memory.  Then, process_file () is called for each name
; in the list.  The process_file () function is user-supplied.  It
; is not part of this library.  If the process_file () function
; detects an error, it should report it and return a nonzero
; value.  This function must be of the form:
;
; word process_file(byte *file_spec).
;
; The reason a list of files is built ahead of time is to prevent
; changes in the disk directory from causing redundant processing.
; Such changes could occur due to the actions of process_file ().
;
; in:   filespec -> filename (can include d:\path and globals)
;
; out:  == 0 if no error, else != 0
;
; errs: insufficient memory to malloc buffer for file list
;       an error from findfirst/findnext other than no more files
;       the case of no files being found for a filespec
;       a !=0 return from process_file()
;
;,fe
==================================================================*/
```

```
#define ld_list_size 2000

word lc_find_files ( byte *filespec )
{

  word first;                    // controls findfirst/next calls
  word err_stat;                 // holds error status
  word name_cnt;                 // detects "no files found" case
  word x;                        // misc counter
  word list_free;                // tracks remaining list space
  struct ffblk ffblk;            // for findfirst/next
  byte drvstr[MAXDRIVE];         // for fnsplit
  byte pathstr[MAXDIR];          // for fnsplit
  byte fnamestr[MAXFILE];        // for fnsplit
  byte extstr[MAXEXT];           // for fnsplit
  byte wbuf[MAXPATH];            // holds d:\path filespec portion
  byte *trunc_ptr;               // used to maintain wbuf
  byte *list_ptr;                // used to manage directory list
  byte *list_base;               // used to manage directory list

  // extract any drive and path preceeding the filename

  fnsplit ( filespec, drvstr, pathstr, fnamestr, extstr );
  strcpy ( wbuf, drvstr );
  strcat ( wbuf, pathstr );
  trunc_ptr = strchr ( wbuf, 0 );
  if ( ( list_base = (byte *) malloc ( ld_list_size ) ) == NULL)  {
    lc_disp_err_lead ( "Insufficient memory\n" );
    return ( 1 );
  }
  list_ptr = list_base;
  list_free = ld_list_size;
  name_cnt = 0;
  first = 1;
  ffblk.ff_attrib = 0;
  while ( 1 ) {

    // find each target file and record its name in the list

    if ( first ) {
      err_stat = findfirst ( filespec, &ffblk, 0 );
    } else {
      err_stat = findnext ( &ffblk );
    }
```

```
     if ( err_stat != 0 ) {
       if ( _doserrno == 0x12 ) {
         break;
       } else {
         lc_disp_err_lead ( "File error in fndfiles ()\n" );
         free ( list_base );
         return ( 1 );
       }
     }
     x = strlen ( ffblk.ff_name ) + 1;
     if ( x > list_free ) return ( 1 );
     strcpy ( list_ptr, ffblk.ff_name );
     list_ptr += x;
     name_cnt++;
     first = 0;
   }
   if ( name_cnt == 0 ) {
     lc_disp_err_lead ( "No files found for filespec: " );
     lc_disp_str ( filespec );
     lc_disp_str ( "\n" );
     free ( list_base );
     return ( 1 );
   }
   list_ptr = list_base;
   for ( x = 0; x < name_cnt; x++ ) {

// combine any original drive and path with the found
// fname.ext and process each file in the list

     *trunc_ptr = 0;
     strcat ( wbuf, list_ptr );
     if ( process_file ( wbuf ) != 0 ) {
       free ( list_base );
       return ( 1 );
     }
     list_ptr += strlen ( list_ptr ) + 1;
   }
   free ( list_base );
   return ( 0 );
}
```

lc_trace_dir()

```
#include <dos.h>
#include <dir.h>
#include <string.h>

#define res 0
#include "\zlib\zlib.h"

/*================================================================
;,fs
; word lc_trace_dir ( byte *dpbuf, fspc_type *fsptr )
;
; This function is effectively the same as lc_trace_dirl (),
; except that no list is built of the filenames found.  This
; function is for the case where the activity of the work
; function includes the building of a list, so that using
; lc_trace_dirl () would involve a waste of time and memory.
;
; See lc_trace_dirl () for other usage notes.
;
;,fe
================================================================*/
word lc_trace_dir ( byte *dpbuf, fspc_type *fsptr )
{

    byte *orig_end;                 // ptr to original end of dpbuf
    byte *trunc_ptr;                // used to maintain wbuf
    struct ffblk ffblk;             // structure for findfirst/next
    word err_stat;                  // holds error status

    // Record the original ending point of the string in the
    // drive/path buffer.  Then make sure it ends with a backslash
    // (unless it's a null string -- for the current directory).

    orig_end = (byte *) strchr ( dpbuf, 0 );
    trunc_ptr = orig_end;
```

```
  if ( orig_end != dpbuf ) {
    if ( *( trunc_ptr - 1 ) != '\\' ) {
      *trunc_ptr = '\\';
      trunc_ptr++;
      *trunc_ptr = 0;
    }
  }
  strcat ( dpbuf, ( fsptr->search_spec ) );

  // find each target file and call the work function

  while ( 1 ) {
    if ( trunc_ptr != NULL ) {
      err_stat = findfirst ( dpbuf, &ffblk, fsptr->search_attr);
      *trunc_ptr = 0;
      trunc_ptr = NULL;
    } else {
      err_stat = findnext ( &ffblk );
    }
    if ( err_stat != 0 ) {
      if ( _doserrno == 0x12 ) {
        break;
      } else {
        *orig_end = 0;
        return ( 2 );
      }
    }

    // For each file found, call the work function with a
    // pointer to dpbuf, the found name and its attribute.

    if ( ( *( fsptr->work_func ) ) ( dpbuf, ffblk.ff_name,
       ffblk.ff_attrib ) != 0 ) {
      *orig_end = 0;
      return ( 4 );
    }
  }
  *orig_end = 0;
  return ( 0 );
}
```

free_lptr_list()

```c
#include <dos.h>
#include <dir.h>
#include <string.h>

#define res 0
#include "\zlib\zlib.h"

//==== internal data structure

static struct fname_type {
  struct fname_type *next;
  byte fname[13];
  byte attr;
};

typedef struct fname_type fntype;

/*===============================================================
; static void free_lptr_list ( fntype *fptr )
;
; in:   fptr -> root of fntype list
;
; out:
;
===============================================================*/
static void free_lptr_list ( fntype *fptr )
{

  fntype *fptr2;
  fntype *fptr3;

  fptr2 = fptr;
  while ( fptr2 != NULL ) {
    fptr3 = fptr2;
    fptr2 = fptr2->next;
    free ( fptr3 );
  }
}
```

lc_trace_dirl()

```
/*================================================================
;,fs
; word lc_trace_dirl ( byte *dpbuf, fspc_type *fsptr )
;
; findfirst () and findnext () are used to build a list of target
; files in memory.  Then, a work function is called for each name
; in the list.  The work function is user-supplied.  It is not
; part of this library.  If the work function detects an error,
; it should report it and return a nonzero value.  This function
; must be of the form
;
; word process_file ( byte *dpstr, byte *fname, byte attr );
;
; where:
; dpstr -> the drive/path portion of the search specification
; fname -> the filename.ext of the found file
; attr = the attribute of the found file
;
; The use of the name "process_file" is merely an example.  Since
; the name of the work function must be passed into this
; function through the fspc_type structure, any valid function
; name may be used.
;
; A list of files is built ahead of time to prevent changes in
; the disk directory from causing redundant processing.  Such
; changes could occur due to the actions of process_file().
;
; IMPORTANT NOTE ON DPBUF:
;
; The dpbuf buffer must contain enough additional storage space
; for the longest possible fname.ext type of search
; specification.  This would be a string of the form
; "????????.???", which requires 13 characters including the
; terminating 0.  Also, if the dpbuf string does not end with a
; backslash, one will be added, so, given that the string in dpbuf
; will already have a terminator, there must always be 13 free
; bytes at the end of this buffer.
;
```

```
; in:    fsptr -> a filled-out fspc_type type of structure
;        dpbuf -> a buffer containing the drive/path portion
;                     of the search specification.  SEE NOTE ABOVE.
;
; out:   retval = 0 means no error
;        retval = 1 means insufficient memory for file list
;        retval = 2 means an error from findfirst/findnext
;                     other than no more files
;        retval = 4 means a != 0 return from the process function
;
;,fe
=================================================================*/
word lc_trace_dirl ( byte *dpbuf, fspc_type *fsptr )
{
  byte *orig_end;                 // ptr to original end of dpbuf
  byte *trunc_ptr;                // used to maintain wbuf
  struct ffblk ffblk              // structure for findfirst/next
  word err_stat;                  // holds error status
  fntype *root_lptr = NULL;       // root of the heap list of fnames
  fntype *lptr = NULL;            // used to build heap list
  fntype *last_lptr;              // used to build heap list

  // Record the original ending point of the string in the
  // drive/path buffer.  Then make sure it ends with a backslash
  // (unless it's a null string -- for the current directory).

  orig_end = (byte *) strchr ( dpbuf, 0 );
  trunc_ptr = orig_end;
  if ( orig_end != dpbuf ) {
    if ( *( trunc_ptr - 1 ) != '\\' ) {
      *trunc_ptr = '\\';
      trunc_ptr++;
      *trunc_ptr = 0;
    }
  }
  strcat ( dpbuf, fsptr->search_spec );
```

```
// find each target file and record its name in the list

while ( 1 ) {

  if ( root_lptr == NULL ) {
    err_stat = findfirst ( dpbuf, &ffblk, fsptr->search_attr);
  } else {
    err_stat = findnext ( &ffblk );
  }
  if ( err_stat != 0 ) {
    if ( _doserrno == 0x12 ) {
      break;
    } else {
      free_lptr_list ( root_lptr );
      *orig_end = 0;
      return ( 2 );
    }
  }

  // allocate a node from the heap and fill in the data

  last_lptr = lptr;
  if ( ( lptr = (fntype *) malloc ( sizeof (fntype) ) ) == NULL ) {
    free_lptr_list ( root_lptr );
    *orig_end = 0;
    return ( 1 );
  }
  lptr->next = NULL;
  strcpy ( lptr->fname, ffblk.ff_name );
  lptr->attr = ffblk.ff_attrib;
  if ( last_lptr == NULL ) {
    root_lptr = lptr;
  } else {
    last_lptr->next = lptr;
  }
}
if ( root_lptr == NULL ) {
  *orig_end = 0;
  return ( 0 );
}
```

```
// Restore dpbuf and then for each found name in the list,
// call the work function with a pointer to dpbuf, the found
// name, and its attribute.

*trunc_ptr = 0;
lptr = root_lptr;
while ( lptr != NULL ) {
  if ( ( *( fsptr->work_func ) ) ( dpbuf, lptr->fname, lptr->attr )
                                                  != 0 ) {
    free_lptr_list ( root_lptr );
    *orig_end = 0;
    return ( 4 );
  }
  lptr = lptr->next;
}
free_lptr_list ( root_lptr );
*orig_end = 0;
return ( 0 );
}
```

lc_tracdir_prep()

```
#include <dir.h>
#include <dos.h>
#include <string.h>

#define res 0
#include "\zlib\zlib.h"

/*================================================================
;,fs
; void lc_tracdir_prep ( byte *input_str, byte *srcpath,
;                                byte *srcfn )
;
; Prepare a filespec string for use with lc_trace_dir () by
; splitting it into a drive/path component and a fname.ext
; component.
;
; in:    input_str -> the string to process
;        srcpath -> buffer where the drive/path component
;         is to be written
;        srcfn -> buffer where the fname.ext component
;         is to be written
;
; out:
;
;,fe
================================================================*/
void lc_tracdir_prep ( byte *input_str, byte *srcpath,
                               byte *srcfn )
{

  byte drvstr[MAXDRIVE];
  byte pathstr[MAXDIR];
  byte fnamestr[MAXFILE];
  byte extstr[MAXEXT];

  fnsplit ( input_str, drvstr, pathstr, fnamestr, extstr );
  strcpy ( srcpath, drvstr );
  strcat ( srcpath, pathstr );
  strupr ( srcpath );
  strcpy ( srcfn, fnamestr );
  strcat ( srcfn, extstr );
}
```

lc_build_tree(), lc_trace_tree(), lc_free_tree()

```
#define res 0
#include "\zlib\zlib.h"

#include <dir.h>
#include <dos.h>
#include <string.h>

// values for the prvt field within the tnode structure

#define DT_PARENT       0
#define DT_SAME         1
#define DT_ROOT         2

/*==================================================================
;,fs
; word lc_build_tree ( byte drvltr, tn_type **root_tnode )
;
; in:   drvltr = drive letter of drive to map (e.g. 'A', 'B'...)
;       root_tnode -> pointer to be used as the root
;
; out:  retval != 0 if error
;
;,fe
=================================================================*/
word lc_build_tree ( byte drvltr, tn_type **root_tnode )
{

    tn_type *cur_tnode;
    tn_type *tptr;
    tn_type *toplvl_tnode;
    byte *trunc_ptr;
    byte first1;
    byte first2;
    byte pathbuf[100];
    word err_stat;
    struct ffblk ffblk;
    byte any_dirs;
```

```
// allocate a tn_type node for root directory

if ( ( cur_tnode = (tn_type *) malloc ( sizeof (tn_type) ) )
                                             == NULL ) {
   return(1);
}
cur_tnode->prvt = DT_ROOT;
cur_tnode->prev = NULL;
cur_tnode->child = NULL;
cur_tnode->next = NULL;
*root_tnode = cur_tnode;

// need both pathbuf and the name field of the first note set
// to the string "?:\"
// (where the '?' is the actual drive letter).

strcpy ( pathbuf, "?:\\" );
pathbuf[0] = drvltr;
strcpy ( cur_tnode->name, pathbuf );

trunc_ptr = (byte *) strchr ( pathbuf, 0 );
first1 = 1;
first2 = 1;
while ( 1 ) {

   // find the first/next directory entry

   if ( first1 ) {
     first1 = 0;
     strcpy ( trunc_ptr, "*.*" );
     any_dirs = 0;
     err_stat = findfirst ( pathbuf, &ffblk, FA_DIREC );
   } else {
     err_stat = findnext ( &ffblk );
   }
   if ( err_stat == 0 ) {

     // bypass dot and dot-dot directory entries

     if ( ( ffblk.ff_attrib & 0x10 ) == 0 ||
       ffblk.ff_name[0] == '.' ) {
       continue;
     }
     any_dirs = 1;
```

```
// allocate new tnode record, fill it out, and
// link it into the tree

if ( ( tptr = (tn_type *) malloc ( sizeof(tn_type) ) )
                                        == NULL ) {
  return(1);
}
if ( first2 ) {
  first2 = 0;
  toplvl_tnode = tptr;
  cur_tnode->child = tptr;
  tptr->prvt = DT_PARENT;
} else {
  cur_tnode->next = tptr;
  tptr->prvt = DT_SAME;
}
tptr->prev = cur_tnode;
tptr->child = NULL;
tptr->next = NULL;
strcpy(tptr->name,ffblk.ff_name);
cur_tnode = tptr;
} else {
if ( _doserrno == 0x12 ) {

  // when no more directories in the current dir

  if ( any_dirs == 0 ) {

    // If the current directory didn't have any child
    // directories, then it's time to advance to a next
    // node or repeal a level.

    while ( 1 ) {

      // scan back with trunc_ptr to find previous
      // backslash, write a 0 after it, and point trunc_ptr
      // to that 0

      if ( *( trunc_ptr - 1 ) == '\\' ) {
        trunc_ptr--;
      }
```

```
          while ( *( trunc_ptr - 1 ) != '\\' ) {
            trunc_ptr--;
          }
          *trunc_ptr = 0;

          // see if can advance a node deeper or if need
          // to repeal

          if ( cur_tnode->next != NULL ) {
            cur_tnode = cur_tnode->next;
            break;
          } else {
            cur_tnode = toplvl_tnode->prev;
            toplvl_tnode = cur_tnode;
            while ( toplvl_tnode->prvt == DT_SAME ) {
              toplvl_tnode = toplvl_tnode->prev;
            }
            if ( toplvl_tnode->prvt == DT_ROOT ) {
              return(0);
            }
          }
        }
      } else {

        // If current directory did have children, go back
        // to the top node of the current level to begin
        // searching for child directories.

        cur_tnode = toplvl_tnode;
      }

      strcpy ( trunc_ptr, cur_tnode->name );
      trunc_ptr = (byte *) strchr ( trunc_ptr, 0);
      *trunc_ptr = '\\';
      trunc_ptr++;
      *trunc_ptr = 0;
      first1 = 1;
      first2 = 1;
    } else {
      return ( 2 );
    }
  }
 }
}
```

```
/*=================================================================
;,fs
; word lc_trace_tree ( tn_type *root_tnode, word (*work_func) (),
;                      void *passthru )
;
; in:   root_tnode -> the first node in the tree
;       work_func -> the work function
;       passthru -> data structure to be used by work function
;
; out:  retval != 0 if error
;
;,fe
=================================================================*/
word lc_trace_tree ( tn_type *root_tnode, word (*work_func) (),
                     void *passthru )
{

  tn_type *cur_tnode;
  word retval;
  byte workbuf[100];
  byte *bptr;

  cur_tnode = root_tnode;
  if ( cur_tnode == NULL ) {
    return ( 0 );
  }
  workbuf[0] = 0;
  while ( 1 ) {
    strcat ( workbuf, cur_tnode->name );
    bptr = (byte *) strchr ( workbuf, 0 ) - 1;
    if ( *bptr != '\\' ) {
      strcat ( workbuf, "\\" );
    }
    retval = (work_func) ( workbuf, passthru );
    if ( retval != 0 ) {
      return ( retval );
    }
```

```
        // whenever there's a child node, go deeper into the tree.

    if ( cur_tnode->child != NULL ) {
      cur_tnode = cur_tnode->child;
    } else {

        // When can't go deeper, process any other nodes at the
        // current depth.  Start by trimming the string in workbuf
        // back one stage.

      while ( 1 ) {
        bptr = (byte *) strchr ( workbuf, 0 ) - 2;
        while ( *bptr != '\\' ) {
          bptr--;
        }
        *( bptr + 1 ) = 0;
        if ( cur_tnode->next != NULL ) {
          cur_tnode = cur_tnode->next;
          break;
        }

          // If no more nodes at current depth, back up to parent
          // and then recycle to top of loop to check for a next
          // node at the parent level.

        while ( cur_tnode->prvt == DT_SAME ) {
          cur_tnode = cur_tnode->prev;
        }
        if ( cur_tnode->prvt == DT_PARENT ) {
          cur_tnode = cur_tnode->prev;
        }
        if ( cur_tnode->prvt == DT_ROOT ) {
          return ( 0 );
        }
      }
    }
  }
}
```

```
/*=================================================================
;,fs
; void lc_free_tree ( tn_type *root_tnode )
;
; in:   root_tnode -> the first node in the tree
;
; out:
;
;,fe
=================================================================*/
void lc_free_tree ( tn_type *root_tnode )
{
  tn_type *cur_tnode;
  tn_type *prev_ptr;
  byte prev_type;
  cur_tnode = root_tnode;
  if ( cur_tnode == NULL ) {
    return;
  }
  while ( 1 ) {

    // Whenever there's a child node, go deeper into the tree.

    if ( cur_tnode->child != NULL ) {
      cur_tnode = cur_tnode->child;
      continue;
    }

    // When can't go deeper, traverse along any nodes at the
    // current depth.

    if ( cur_tnode->next != NULL ) {
      cur_tnode = cur_tnode->next;
      continue;
    }
```

```
    // When no child and no next, found a node that can be freed.

    prev_type = cur_tnode->prvt;
    rev_ptr = cur_tnode->prev;
    free ( cur_tnode );
    cur_tnode = prev_ptr;

    // Figure out how to backtrace.

    if ( prev_type == DT_SAME ) {
      cur_tnode->next = NULL;
      continue;
    }
    if ( prev_type == DT_PARENT ) {
      cur_tnode->child = NULL;
      continue;
    }

    // when prev_type isn't same or parent, must be root

    free ( cur_tnode );
    return;
  }
}
```

lc_eat_key()

```
#include <stdlib.h>
#include <conio.h>

#define res 0
#include "\zlib\zlib.h"

/*===============================================================
;,fs
; void lc_eat_key ( void )
;
; Flush any keys in the type-ahead buffer.
;
; in:
;
; out:
;
;,fe
===============================================================*/
void lc_eat_key ( void )
{

  byte t;

  while ( lc_ifkey () ) {
    t = lc_getkey ();
  }
}
```

lc_getkey_set()

```c
#include <stdlib.h>
#include <string.h>
#include <ctype.h>

#define res 0
#include "\zlib\zlib.h"

/*================================================================
;,fs
; byte lc_getkey_set ( byte *xset )
;
; Wait until a keystroke is pressed that is within the specified
; set of characters, beeping for other characters.  The keystroke
; is not echoed to the screen.  Extended keycodes are converted
; to single-byte values above 0x80 (by lc_getkey).  Alpha keys
; are internally converted to upper case.  See the defined values
; in zlib.h.
;
; in:
;
; out:  the keycode of the key that was pressed
;
;,fe
================================================================*/
byte lc_getkey_set ( byte *xset )
{

  byte key;

  while ( 1 ) {
    key = toupper ( lc_getkey () );
    if ( key != 0 && strchr ( xset, key ) != NULL )  {
      return ( key );
    }
    lc_beep ();
  }
}
```

lc_beep()

```
#include <stdlib.h>
#include <dos.h>

#define res 0
#include "\zlib\zlib.h"

/*================================================================
;,fs
; void lc_beep ( void )
;
; Make the speaker beep.
;
; in:
;
; out:
;
;,fe
================================================================*/
void lc_beep ( void )
{

  byte t;

  sound ( 440 );
  delay ( 30 );
  nosound ();
}
```

lc_set_phook(), lc_set_fhook(), lc_set_ahook(), lc_getkey(),
lc_ifkey()

```c
#include <stdlib.h>
#include <conio.h>

#define res 0
#include "\zlib\zlib.h"

static byte dummy_poll ( void );
static byte dummy_filter ( byte t );
static byte dummy_avail ( void );

static byte (*poll_hook) () = dummy_poll;
static byte (*filter_hook) () = dummy_filter;
static byte (*avail_hook) () = dummy_avail;

static byte dummy_poll ( void ) {
  return ( 0 );
}

static byte dummy_filter ( byte t ) {
  return(0);
}

static byte dummy_avail ( void ) {
  return ( 0 );
}

/*================================================================
;,fs
; void lc_set_phook ( byte (*new_poll_func) ())
;
; Establishes a poll function for lc_getkey (). Useful for
; background processing.
;
; in:  new_poll_func -> poll function
;
; out:
;
;,fe
================================================================*/
```

```c
void lc_set_phook ( byte (*new_poll_func) () )
{
  poll_hook = new_poll_func;
}


/*===============================================================
;,fs
; void lc_set_fhook ( byte (*new_filter_func) () )
;
; Establishes a filter function for lc_getkey ().  Useful for
; hot key support.
;
; in:   new_filter_func -> filter function
;
; out:
;
;,fe
===============================================================*/
void lc_set_fhook ( byte (*new_filter_func) () )
{

  filter_hook = new_filter_func;
}


/*===============================================================
;,fs
; void lc_set_ahook ( byte (*new_avail_func) () )
;
; Establishes an avail function for lc_getkey ().  Use in
; conjunction with a poll hook that supplies emulation data.
; Allows the availability of emulation data to be known to
; lc_ifkey ().
;
; in:   new_avail_func -> avail function
;
; out:
;
;,fe
===============================================================*/
void lc_set_ahook ( byte (*new_avail_func) () )
{

  avail_hook = new_avail_func;
}
```

```
/*==================================================================
;,fs
; byte lc_getkey (void)
;
; Wait until a keystroke is pressed.  The keystroke is not echoed
; to the screen.  Extended keycodes are converted to single-byte
; values above 0x80.  See the defined values in keydefs.h.
;
; in:
;
; out:  the keycode of the key that was pressed
;
;,fe
=================================================================*/
byte lc_getkey ( void )
{

   byte t;

   while ( 1 ) {
     t = (*poll_hook) ();
     if ( t == 0 ) {
       if( kbhit () ) {
         t = getch ();
         if ( t == 0 ) {
           t = getch ();
           if ( t < 0x80 ) {
             t += 0x80;
           } else

             // special-case logic for cntrl-pgup,
             // alt-9, alt-0, alt--, and alt-=

             if ( t > 0x84 ) {
             t = 0;
             }
           }
         }
       } else {
         continue;
       }
     }
```

```
      if ( (*filter_hook) ( &t)  == 0 ) {
        break;
      }
    }
  return(t);
}

/*================================================================
;,fs
; byte lc_ifkey ( void )
;
;
; in:
;
; out:  retval != 0 if a key, else retval = 0
;
;,fe
================================================================*/
byte lc_ifkey ( void ) {

  if ( (*avail_hook) () ) {
    return ( 1 );
  }
  return ( kbhit () );
}
```

lc_process_src_parms()

```
#include <stdio.h>
#include <string.h>

#define res 0
#include "\zlib\zlib.h"

/*===================================================================
;,fs
; word lc_process_src_parms ( byte *p_line, word (*wrk_fun) ())
;
; This function would be used to process a buffer of fixed-type
; parameters, as an alternative to lc_parse_fx (). Each parameter
; is expected to be a source file specification and may contain a
; drive/path component and/or wildcards. A parameter starting
; with a # character is treated as the name of a file that
; contains a list of filespecs.
;
; The work function is passed to lc_trace_dirl (). See the
; documentation for that function for more details.
;
; in:   p_line -> unified parameter line of source filespecs
;       wrk_fun -> the work function for lc_trace_dirl()
;
; out:  == 0 if no error, else != 0
;
; errs: a file preceeded by a '#' cannot be opened.
;       a non-zero return from fnd_files().
;
;,fe
====================================================================*/

#define LD_PRSCBUF 80

word lc_process_src_parms ( byte *p_line, word (*wrk_fun) () )
{

  byte workbuf[LD_PRSCBUF];      // line buffer for #fname case
  byte *wptr;                    // use to process strings in workbuf
```

```
byte *tok_ptr;               // use with strtok ()
FILE *source;                // file pointer for #fname case
fspc_type ffx;               // lc_trace_dirl () entry parm
byte srcpath[81];            // lc_trace_dirl () entry parm
byte srcfn[13];              // lc_trace_dirl () entry parm
word retval;                 // holds lc_trace_dirl () return value

// prepare record for lc_trace_dirl ()

ffx.work_func = wrk_fun;
ffx.search_attr = 0;
ffx.search_spec = srcfn;

// for each file specification in the entry string

tok_ptr = strtok ( p_line, " \t" );
while ( tok_ptr != NULL ) {

  // if the file spec starts with a '#', open the file

  if ( *tok_ptr == '#' ) {
    tok_ptr++;
    if ( ( source = fopen ( tok_ptr, "r" ) ) == NULL ) {
      lc_disp_err_lead ( "Opening source file: " );
      lc_disp_str ( tok_ptr );
      lc_disp_str ( "\n" );
      return ( 1 );
    }

    // read each file spec from the #file

    while ( feof ( source ) == 0 ) {
      if ( ( fgets ( workbuf, LD_PRSCBUF, source ) ) == NULL) {
        break;
      }
      wptr = workbuf;
      lc_trim_parm ( &wptr );
      if ( *wptr == ';' || *wptr == 0 ) {
        continue;
      }
```

```
        // call lc_trace_dirl () with the file spec

        lc_tracdir_prep ( wptr, srcpath, srcfn );
        retval = lc_trace_dirl ( srcpath, &ffx );
        if ( retval ) {
          return ( 1 );
        }
      }
      fclose ( source );
    } else {

        // call lc_trace_dirl() with the file spec

        lc_tracdir_prep ( tok_ptr, srcpath, srcfn );
        retval = lc_trace_dirl ( srcpath, &ffx );
        if( retval ) {
          return ( 1 );
        }
    }
    tok_ptr = strtok ( NULL, " \t" );
  }
  return ( 0 );
}
```

`lc_home_path()`

```
#define res 0
#include "\zlib\zlib.h"

/*=================================================================
;,fs
; void lc_home_path ( byte *bufptr, word psp_seg )
;
; Extract the drive and path from which a program was loaded.
; Useful when companion files must be located.  Note: This
; function must not be used with a pre-3.x version of DOS.
;
; in:   bufptr -> buffer for resulting string
;       psp_seg = the segment of the psp
;
; out:  buffer at bufptr filled with home path string,
;       ending with a '\'
;
;,fe
=================================================================*/
void lc_home_path ( byte *strngptr, word psp_seg )
{

   dword eptr;
   byte  *holdptr;

   // make eptr point to the start of the environment

   SETDWORD( eptr, psp_seg, 0x2c );
   DSEG( eptr ) = *eptr.wptr;
   DOFS( eptr ) = 0;

   // find the end of the first section

   while ( *eptr.wptr != 0 ) {
     eptr.bptr++;
   }
   eptr.bptr += 4;
   while ( *eptr.bptr != 0 ) {
     *strngptr = *eptr.bptr;
     eptr.bptr++;
     if ( *strngptr++ == '\' ) holdptr = strngptr;
   }
   *holdptr = 0;
}
```

lc_form_template(), lc_translate_template()

```c
#include <dos.h>

#define res 0
#include "\zlib\zlib.h"

/*================================================================
;,fs
; byte lc_form_template ( byte *filespec, byte *template )
;
; call int21 func 29 to parse a filespec into normalized form.
;
; NOTE: This function makes use of an INT21 function call.
; Use of this function within a TSR or device driver requires
; care.
;
; in:    filespec -> fname.ext (with wildcards)
;        template -> 11 byte buffer for resulting template
;
; out:   retval = 0 if no error and no wildcard characters
;          *template -> parsed version of non-wild filespec
;        retval = 1 if no error and wildcard characters found
;          *template -> parsed version wildcard type filespec
;        retval = 0xff if error
;          *template -> undefined
;
;,fe
=================================================================*/
byte lc_form_template ( byte *filespec, byte *template )
{

   union REGS regs; struct SREGS sregs;
   byte fcb[37];

   memset ( fcb,0,37 );
   regs.x.ax = 0x2903;
   regs.x.si = (word) filespec;
   sregs.ds = _DS;
```

```
    regs.x.di = (word) &fcb[0];
    sregs.es = _DS;
    int86x ( 0x21, &regs, &regs, &sregs );
    memcpy ( template, &fcb[1],11 );
    return ( regs.h.al );
}


/*================================================================
;,fs
; word lc_translate_template ( byte *in_filespec,
;                                  byte *out_filespec, byte *template)
;
; Parse the found file name and process it through
; the template to derive the final target name.
;
; NOTE: This function makes use of an INT21 function call.
; Use of this function within a TSR or device driver requires
; care.
;
; in:   in_filespec -> the found filename (read only)
;       out_filespec -> buffer for result (written to)
;       template -> translation template  (read only)
;
; out:  retval = 0 if no error
;        translated filespec written at *out_filespec
;       retval != 0 if error
;
;,fe
================================================================*/
word lc_translate_template ( byte *in_filespec,
                                byte *out_filespec, byte *template)
{

    word x;
    word w;
    byte t2[11];
    byte result[11];
```

```c
if ( lc_form_template ( in_filespec, t2 ) == 0xff ) {
  return ( 1 );
}
memcpy ( &result[0], template, 11 );
for ( x = 0; x < 11; x++ ) {
  if ( template[x] == '?' )  {
    result[x] = t2[x];
  }
}
x = 7;
while ( result[x--] == ' ' );
x += 2;
memcpy ( out_filespec, &result[0], x );
*( out_filespec + x ) = '.';
w = 10;
while ( (w > 7 ) && ( result[w--] == ' ' ) );
if ( (w == 7 ) && ( result[8] == ' ' ) )  {
*( out_filespec + x + 1 ) = 0;
}
else {
  memcpy ( ( out_filespec + x + 1 ), &result[8], ( w - 6 ) );
  *( out_filespec + x + 1 + ( w - 6 ) ) = 0;
}
return ( 0 );
}
```

lc_subst_meta()

```
#include <string.h>

#define res 0
#include "\zlib\zlib.h"

/*==================================================================
;,fs
; word lc_subst_meta ( byte *src, byte *wrk, word maxlen,
;                      byte *meta, byte *new )
;
; This function scans the source string for a metastring.  If
; found, it is replaced with the specified new string.  For
; example, given the source string "the cat is #. fat", the
; metastring "#." and the new string "very", the result would be
; "the cat is very fat".
;
; in:   src -> string to process
;           (in buffer with room for new string)
;       wrk -> scratch buffer (must be at least as large as src)
;       maxlen = allocation size of src
;       meta -> metastring
;       new -> replacement substring
;
; out:  != 0 if final string would be longer than maxlen
;
;,fe
================================================================*/
word lc_subst_meta ( byte *src, byte *wrk, word maxlen,
                     byte *meta, byte *new )
{

    byte *xptr;
    byte *yptr;
    word ml;
    word nl;
```

```
    while ( (xptr = strstr ( src, meta ) ) != NULL) {
      ml = strlen ( meta );
      nl = strlen ( new );
      if ( ( strlen ( src ) - ml + nl + 1) > maxlen ) return ( 1);
      strcpy ( wrk, xptr + ml);
      strcpy ( xptr, new);
      strcpy (xptr + nl, wrk);
    }
    return ( 0 );
}
```

On the Companion Diskette

The Companion Diskette contains the templates and library functions discussed in this book. The disk's directory structure is as follows:

```
\ZLIB                   Common files: .H, .INC, .LIB
\ZLIB\BATCH             Batch files
\ZLIB\EXECUTE           Executable binary modules
\ZLIB\WORK              Main working directory
\ZLIB\WORK\STOCK        Template files
\ZLIB\WORK\TEST         Test programs
\ZLIB\LIBSRC            Library source
```

See the READ.ME file in the root directory for more details.

INSTALLING THE COMPANION TOOLSET

To install this Companion Toolset on a hard disk, use DOS's XCOPY command as follows:

```
xcopy a: c:\  /s
```

265

This installation process will result in a copy of this READ.ME file existing within the root directory. Since another copy of this file does exist within the \ZLIB directory, you may wish to delete the one in the root directory.

Next, add C:\ZLIB\EXECUTE and C:\ZLIB\BATCH to your command search path (presuming installation on drive C:).

If you wish to install this package on a different drive (such as D: or E:), you will need to edit and rename certain files. See the READ.ME file for details. The READ.ME file also lists the files that contain compiler-specific commands.

INDEX

.EXE file, 18, 24, 25, 28, 42, 46, 48, 72
.LIB file, 24, 32, 49, 101
.MAK file, 47, 48, 73–74, 101–103, 112–114
.MAP file, 18
.OBJ file, 22, 24–25, 28, 32–34, 40, 46, 77, 101
.SYS file, 46, 48, 72
_BSS, *see* Segments, code and data
_DATA, *see* Segments, code and data
_TEXT, *see* Segments, code and data
80286, *see* CPU
80386, *see* CPU
80486, *see* CPU
8080, *see* CPU
8085, *see* CPU
8086, *see* CPU
80X86, *see* CPU
8253 clock chip, 56

A

Abstraction, 87–91
Action charts, *see* Pseudocode, action charts
Addressing, stack, *see* Stack, addressing
ASM, 37–44, 51, 76

ASMTYPES.H, 175
Assembler, 22, 24
Assembly language, *see* ASM

B

BIOS, 11
BRIEF, 122

C

Cdecl, 100
Central processing unit, *see* CPU
CLC.BAT, 48
CLEANTXT.C, 142
CLEANTXT.EXE, 116–117, 142
Code segment, *see* Segments, code and data
Cohesion, 9
COMDEF, 26–27
COMMENT, 26–27
Comment header block, 107–109
Compiler, 22, 24, 100. *See also* CLC.BAT
    preprocessor, 17–18
Console input processing, 128–137
    console stack, 135
    hooks, 95–98, 130–132, 136
    macros, 133

Console input
processing *(continued)*
mouse emulation, 133, 135
multiple threads, 135–136
Coupling, 9
CPU, 57–58

D

Data segment, *see* Segments, code
and data
DDHEADER.INC, 73
DDHSTOCK.INC, 45–46
DDRSTOCK.C, 45–46
DDSTOCK.MAK, 45–46, 73, 77
DDSTRTUP.ASM, 45–46, 70,
72–73, 75, 76, 78
DDSTRUCS.H, 75
DDTSTOCK.C, 45–46, 75
Debugging information, 18, 26
Device driver, 5–6, 31, 32–35,
39, 41, 72–76. *See also*
Resident/nonresident code
DGROUP, *see* Segments, code
and data
Directory processing, 147–166. *See
also* File processing; Tree
processing
list building, 151–153
Direct video, 11, 93–95
DLL, *see* Library, dynamic link
Documentation, maintenance
of, 105
DOS, *see* Operating system
system calls, *see* INT21
Dynamic link libraries, *see* Library,
dynamic link

E

Encapsulation, 87–91
EXEC function, 2

EXTDEF, 26–27, 28, 30
Extern, 90. *See also* LEXTRN;
EXTDEF
EXTRACT.EXE, 106–114
parameters, 109–112,
116–118, 127

F

File processing, 139–146. *See also*
Directory processing; Tree
processing
FILT1.C, 166
Filters, 11–15, 165–166
findfirst/findnext,
147–148
Fixup overflow, 25
FIXUPP, 26–27
Functions:
header blocks, 108–109
hook, *see* Hook functions

G

GENNDX.BAT, 114
Getkeys, *see* Console input
processing
GETKEYS.C, 133
GETSTOCK.BAT, 46–47, 73
Global variables, 9–10, 19. *See also*
Private global variables;
Public global variables
Granularity, 18, 91
GRPDEF, 26–27

H

Header files, 99–100
High-level language, *see* HLL
HLL, 31, 37–44, 52, 54–55,
72, 77

Home-path technique, 128
Hook functions, 83, 92–98. *See also*
    Console input processing,
    hooks; Library, functions,
    shell processes

I

Include file libraries, *see* Library,
    include file
Include statement placement,
    18–19
INDOS flag, 60
Information hiding, 87–91
INT01, 57–58
INT08, 3, 56, 60
INT09, 3, 56
INT10, 59, 93
INT16, 3
INT17, 3
INT1C, 3, 60
INT21, 60, 70, 147
Interrupt, *see specific types*
    guarding, 57–58
    handler, 56–57
    intercept, 3, 56–63, 66–69, 70
    reentrance, 58–62
    vector, 21
IRQ0, *see* INT08
IRQ1, *see* INT09

K

KEYDEFS.H, 133

L

LA_ADJLSTK, 64–65
LA_GPCSH, 52
LA_LOCAL_CONTEXT, 52,
    63–64, 66, 68–69, 78

LA_MACS.INC, 50, 51
LA_ORIG_CONTEXT, 52, 65,
    68–69, 78
LA_SETLSTK, 77
Lcall macro, 49–50, 51–53, 99
LC_BUILD_TREE(), 155, 158,
    159
LC_DISP_CHAR(), 76
LC_DISP_ERR_LEAD(), 76
LC_DISP_STR(), 76
LC_EAT_KEY(), 132
LC_FORM_TEMPLATE(),
    162–165
LC_FREE_TREE(), 155, 161
LC_GETKEY(), 132–133, 136
LC_GETKEY_SET(), 132
LC_HOME_PATH(), 128
LC_IFKEY(), 132, 136
LC_ISEMPTY(), 124–125
LC_PARSE_FX, 124–125,
    126–127
LC_PARSE_SW, 124–126
LC_PROCESS_SRC_PARMS,
    153–155
LC_SET_AHOOK(), 132
LC_SET_FHOOK(), 132
LC_SET_PHOOK(), 132
LC_TRACE_DIR(), 149–153
LC_TRACE_TREE(), 149,
    158, 160
LC_TRANSLATE_TEMPLATE(),
    162–165
LEDATA, 26–27, 30
LEXTRN, 51, 77
LGPCALL, 51–52
LIB.EXE, 101
Library:
    design, 81–104
    dynamic link, 22
    functions:
        candidates, 81–82
        error handling, 86–87
        layering, 82
        parameters, 84–85

Library *(continued)*
    prefixes, 83–84, 99
    shell processes, 83, 148–151
    testing, 98–99
  generation, 100–101
  include file, 17–19
  link order control, *see* Link order
    control
  maintenance, 101–102
  resident, 19–22
  standard, 37, 39
  static-link, 22, 24–25, 32
LIDATA, 26–27
LINK.EXE, *see* Linking process
Linking process, 24–25, 27–35,
    37–44, 49–50
Link order control, 5, 31–35,
    48–51, 72, 77, 99, 101
LINNUM, 26–27
LNAME, 26–27, 99

M

Make utility, *see* .MAK file
MDD.BAT, 48, 73
ME.BAT, 48
Mixed language development,
    40–44, 72
MODEND, 26–27, 30
MODOBJ.EXE, 46, 72, 77, 99, 101
Modular functions, 6–10
Mouse support, *see* Console
    input processing, mouse
    emulation
MS-DOS, *see* Operating system

N

NMI, 56, 57
Nonresident code, *see*
    Resident/nonresident code

O

Object module records, 25–31.
    See also .OBJ file
Operating system, 2, 5, 70, 72
OS/2, 22
Overlay modules, 20–21

P

Parameter parsing, *see* Parsing
Parsing, 76, 115–128
  calling, 124–127
  defaults, 127–128
  fixed position, 115–116,
    124–125, 126–127
  multiple filespecs, 116–117
  recognition functions, 118,
    126, 127
  setup, 119–124
  switches, 117–119, 124–126
PARSTEST.C, 118
Pascal, 100
PC-DOS, *see* Operating system
Pipelining, *see* Pipes
Pipes, 11–15
Preprocessor, *see* Compiler,
    preprocessor
Private global variables, 19,
    88–90
Private helper functions, 91–92
Pseudocode, 167–193
  action charts, 167–173
  comment headers, 188–190
  data declarations, 173–180
  function declarations, 169–170,
    180–182
  operators, 182–186
  pointers, 177–180
  translation, 190–193
PUBDEF records (in .OBJ file),
    26–27, 28, 30

Public global variables, 90–91
Public statements, 88, 92. *See also*
    PUBDEF
PUTDISP.C, 76

R

RBSS, *see* Segments, code
    and data
RDATA, *see* Segments, code
    and data
Recognition function, *see* Parsing,
    recognition functions
Redirection, 11–15
regset structure, 63, 67
Resident libraries, *see* Library,
    resident
Resident/nonresident code, 4–5, 6,
    31, 32–35, 48–51, 51–53,
    72, 73, 75. *See also* Device
    driver; TSR
reslib, 50, 51
Reusable functions, 6–10
RTEXT, *see* Segments, code
    and data

S

SEGDEF, 26–27
Segments, code and data,
    48–50, 51–53, 75, 77
Shell processes, *see* Library,
    functions, shell
    processes
Single-step interrupt,
    see INT01
Stack:
    addressing, 53–56
    automatic guarding, 57
    block sizing, 66, 70
    pocket, 70, 71–72

switching, 52, 56–70, 77–79. *See
    also* LA_LOCAL_CONTEXT;
    LA_ORIG_CONTEXT
STANDA.ASM, 45–46
Standalone utility, 1–3, 14–15, 50
Standard error, *see* stderr
Standard input, *see* stdin
Standard library, *see* Library,
    standard
Standard output, *see* stdout
STANDC.C, 45–47
Startup code, 4, 37–38, 42–43
Static-link libraries, *see* Library,
    static-link
Static storage class, 55, 88–89, 92
stderr, 11
stdin, 11–15
stdout, 11–15
Switch parameters, *see* Parsing,
    switches

T

TDUMP.EXE, 25
Templates, 45–48, 72, 73, 75, 77
Terminate and stay resident,
    see TSR
Testing, *see* Library, functions,
    testing
THEADR, 26–27, 30
Timer interrupt, *see* INT08;
    INT1C
TLIBDEFS.H, 99
TLIB.EXE, 101
TPA, 2, 3, 4, 19–21
Transient program area, *see* TPA
Tree processing, 155–162. *See also*
    Directory processing; File
    processing
TSR, 3–5, 31, 32–35, 39, 41,
    70–72. *See also* Resident/
    nonresident code

TSR.ASM, 45–48
TYPDEF, 26–27

U

Unresolved external, 25, 27–28

W

Wildcard processing, 162–165
WILDXFR2.C, 162
WILDXFRM.C, 162
Windows, 22–23

X

XLIBDISP.INC, 76
XPRINT.C, 142

Z

ZLIB.DAT, 114
ZLIBDEFS.H, 51
ZLIB.H, 99
ZLIB.INC, 67, 68, 72
ZLIB.NDX, 76
ZLIB.XXX, 112